Life Application Bible Studies
JAMES

APPLICATION® BIBLE STUDIES

Part 1:
Complete text of James with study notes and features from the
Life Application Study Bible

Part 2:
Thirteen lessons for individual or group study

Study questions written and edited by

Rev. Michael R. Marcey
Rev. David R. Veerman
Dr. James C. Galvin
Dr. Bruce B. Barton

james

New Living Translation®

Tyndale House Publishers, Inc.
Carol Stream, Illinois

Visit Tyndale's exciting Web sites at www.newlivingtranslation.com and www.tyndale.com.

TYNDALE, New Living Translation, NLT, the New Living Translation logo, and *Life Application* are registered trademarks of Tyndale House Publishers, Inc.

Life Application Bible Studies: James

Life Application notes and features copyright © 1988, 1989, 1990, 1991, 1993, 1996, 2004 by Tyndale House Publishers, Inc., Carol Stream, Illinois 60188.

ISBN 978-1-4143-2560-6
Printed in the United States of America

16 15
9 8 7 6 5 4

CONTENTS

A NOTE TO READERS

The *Holy Bible,* New Living Translation, was first published in 1996. It quickly became one of the most popular Bible translations in the English-speaking world. While the NLT's influence was rapidly growing, the Bible Translation Committee determined that an additional investment in scholarly review and text refinement could make it even better. So shortly after its initial publication, the committee began an eight-year process with the purpose of increasing the level of the NLT's precision without sacrificing its easy-to-understand quality. This second-generation text was completed in 2004 and is reflected in this edition of the New Living Translation. An additional update with minor changes was subsequently introduced in 2007.

The goal of any Bible translation is to convey the meaning and content of the ancient Hebrew, Aramaic, and Greek texts as accurately as possible to contemporary readers. The challenge for our translators was to create a text that would communicate as clearly and powerfully to today's readers as the original texts did to readers and listeners in the ancient biblical world. The resulting translation is easy to read and understand, while also accurately communicating the meaning and content of the original biblical texts. The NLT is a general-purpose text especially good for study, devotional reading, and reading aloud in worship services.

We believe that the New Living Translation—which combines the latest biblical scholarship with a clear, dynamic writing style—will communicate God's word powerfully to all who read it. We publish it with the prayer that God will use it to speak his timeless truth to the church and the world in a fresh, new way.

The Publishers
October 2007

INTRODUCTION TO THE
NEW LIVING TRANSLATION

Translation Philosophy and Methodology

English Bible translations tend to be governed by one of two general translation theories. The first theory has been called "formal-equivalence," "literal," or "word-for-word" translation. According to this theory, the translator attempts to render each word of the original language into English and seeks to preserve the original syntax and sentence structure as much as possible in translation. The second theory has been called "dynamic-equivalence," "functional-equivalence," or "thought-for-thought" translation. The goal of this translation theory is to produce in English the closest natural equivalent of the message expressed by the original-language text, both in meaning and in style.

Both of these translation theories have their strengths. A formal-equivalence translation preserves aspects of the original text—including ancient idioms, term consistency, and original-language syntax—that are valuable for scholars and professional study. It allows a reader to trace formal elements of the original-language text through the English translation. A dynamic-equivalence translation, on the other hand, focuses on translating the message of the original-language text. It ensures that the meaning of the text is readily apparent to the contemporary reader. This allows the message to come through with immediacy, without requiring the reader to struggle with foreign idioms and awkward syntax. It also facilitates serious study of the text's message and clarity in both devotional and public reading.

The pure application of either of these translation philosophies would create translations at opposite ends of the translation spectrum. But in reality, all translations contain a mixture of these two philosophies. A purely formal-equivalence translation would be unintelligible in English, and a purely dynamic-equivalence translation would risk being unfaithful to the original. That is why translations shaped by dynamic-equivalence theory are usually quite literal when the original text is relatively clear, and the translations shaped by formal-equivalence theory are sometimes quite dynamic when the original text is obscure.

The translators of the New Living Translation set out to render the message of the original texts of Scripture into clear, contemporary English. As they did so, they kept the concerns of both formal-equivalence and dynamic-equivalence in mind. On the one hand, they translated as simply and literally as possible when that approach yielded an accurate, clear, and natural English text. Many words and phrases were rendered literally and consistently into English, preserving essential literary and rhetorical devices, ancient metaphors, and word choices that give structure to the text and provide echoes of meaning from one passage to the next.

On the other hand, the translators rendered the message more dynamically when the literal rendering was hard to understand, was misleading, or yielded archaic or foreign wording. They clarified difficult metaphors and terms to aid in the reader's understanding. The translators first struggled with the meaning of the words and phrases in the ancient context; then they rendered the message into clear, natural English. Their goal was to be both faithful to the ancient texts and eminently readable. The result is a translation that is both exegetically accurate and idiomatically powerful.

Translation Process and Team

To produce an accurate translation of the Bible into contemporary English, the translation team needed the skills necessary to enter into the thought patterns of the ancient authors and then to render their ideas, connotations, and effects into clear, contemporary English.

To begin this process, qualified biblical scholars were needed to interpret the meaning of the original text and to check it against our base English translation. In order to guard against personal and theological biases, the scholars needed to represent a diverse group of evangelicals who would employ the best exegetical tools. Then to work alongside the scholars, skilled English stylists were needed to shape the text into clear, contemporary English.

With these concerns in mind, the Bible Translation Committee recruited teams of scholars that represented a broad spectrum of denominations, theological perspectives, and backgrounds within the worldwide evangelical community. Each book of the Bible was assigned to three different scholars with proven expertise in the book or group of books to be reviewed. Each of these scholars made a thorough review of a base translation and submitted suggested revisions to the appropriate Senior Translator. The Senior Translator then reviewed and summarized these suggestions and proposed a first-draft revision of the base text. This draft served as the basis for several additional phases of exegetical and stylistic committee review. Then the Bible Translation Committee jointly reviewed and approved every verse of the final translation.

Throughout the translation and editing process, the Senior Translators and their scholar teams were given a chance to review the editing done by the team of stylists. This ensured that exegetical errors would not be introduced late in the process and that the entire Bible Translation Committee was happy with the final result. By choosing a team of qualified scholars and skilled stylists and by setting up a process that allowed their interaction throughout the process, the New Living Translation has been refined to preserve the essential formal elements of the original biblical texts, while also creating a clear, understandable English text.

The New Living Translation was first published in 1996. Shortly after its initial publication, the Bible Translation Committee began a process of further committee review and translation refinement. The purpose of this continued revision was to increase the level of precision without sacrificing the text's easy-to-understand quality. This second-edition text was completed in 2004, and an additional update with minor changes was subsequently introduced in 2007. This printing of the New Living Translation reflects the updated 2007 text.

Written to Be Read Aloud

It is evident in Scripture that the biblical documents were written to be read aloud, often in public worship (see Nehemiah 8; Luke 4:16-20; 1 Timothy 4:13; Revelation 1:3). It is still the case today that more people will hear the Bible read aloud in church than are likely to read it for themselves. Therefore, a new translation must communicate with clarity and power when it is read publicly. Clarity was a primary goal for the NLT translators, not only to facilitate private reading and understanding, but also to ensure that it would be excellent for public reading and make an immediate and powerful impact on any listener.

The Texts behind the New Living Translation

The Old Testament translators used the Masoretic Text of the Hebrew Bible as represented in *Biblia Hebraica Stuttgartensia* (1977), with its extensive system of textual notes; this is an update of Rudolf Kittel's *Biblia Hebraica* (Stuttgart, 1937). The translators also further compared the Dead Sea Scrolls, the Septuagint and other Greek manuscripts, the Samaritan Pentateuch, the Syriac Peshitta, the Latin Vulgate, and any other versions or manuscripts that shed light on the meaning of difficult passages.

The New Testament translators used the two standard editions of the Greek New Testament: the *Greek New Testament*, published by the United Bible Societies (UBS, fourth revised edition, 1993), and *Novum Testamentum Graece*, edited by Nestle and Aland (NA, twenty-seventh edition, 1993). These two editions, which have the same text but differ in punctuation and textual notes, represent, for the most part, the best in modern textual scholarship. However, in cases where strong textual or other scholarly evidence supported the decision, the translators sometimes chose to differ from the UBS and NA Greek texts and followed variant readings found in other ancient witnesses. Significant textual variants of this sort are always noted in the textual notes of the New Living Translation.

Translation Issues

The translators have made a conscious effort to provide a text that can be easily understood by the typical reader of modern English. To this end, we sought to use only vocabulary and language structures in common use today. We avoided using language likely to become quickly dated or that reflects only a narrow subdialect of English, with the goal of making the New Living Translation as broadly useful and timeless as possible.

But our concern for readability goes beyond the concerns of vocabulary and sentence structure. We are also concerned about historical and cultural barriers to understanding the Bible, and we have sought to translate terms shrouded in history and culture in ways that can be immediately understood. To this end:

- We have converted ancient weights and measures (for example, "ephah" [a unit of dry volume] or "cubit" [a unit of length]) to modern English (American) equivalents, since the ancient measures are not generally meaningful to today's readers. Then in the textual footnotes we offer the literal Hebrew, Aramaic, or Greek measures, along with modern metric equivalents.

- Instead of translating ancient currency values literally, we have expressed them in common terms that communicate the message. For example, in the Old Testament, "ten shekels of silver" becomes "ten pieces of silver" to convey the intended message. In the New Testament, we have often translated the "denarius" as "the normal daily wage" to facilitate understanding. Then a footnote offers: "Greek *a denarius*, the payment for a full day's wage." In general, we give a clear English rendering and then state the literal Hebrew, Aramaic, or Greek in a textual footnote.

- Since the names of Hebrew months are unknown to most contemporary readers, and since the Hebrew lunar calendar fluctuates from year to year in relation to the solar calendar used today, we have looked for clear ways to communicate the time of year the Hebrew months (such as Abib) refer to. When an expanded or interpretive rendering is given in the text, a textual note gives the literal rendering. Where it is possible to define a specific ancient date in terms of our modern calendar, we use modern dates in the text. A textual footnote then gives the literal Hebrew date and states the rationale for our rendering. For example, Ezra 6:15 pinpoints the date when the postexilic Temple was completed in Jerusalem: "the third day of the month Adar." This was during the sixth year of King Darius's reign (that is, 515 B.C.). We have translated that date as March 12, with a footnote giving the Hebrew and identifying the year as 515 B.C.

- Since ancient references to the time of day differ from our modern methods of denoting time, we have used renderings that are instantly understandable to the modern reader. Accordingly, we have rendered specific times of day by using approximate equivalents in terms of our common "o'clock" system. On occasion, translations such as "at dawn the next morning" or "as the sun was setting" have been used when the biblical reference is more general.

- When the meaning of a proper name (or a wordplay inherent in a proper name) is relevant to the message of the text, its meaning is often illuminated with a textual footnote. For example, in Exodus 2:10 the text reads: "The princess named him Moses, for she explained, 'I lifted him out of the water.'" The accompanying footnote reads: "*Moses* sounds like a Hebrew term that means 'to lift out.'"

  Sometimes, when the actual meaning of a name is clear, that meaning is included in parentheses within the text itself. For example, the text at Genesis 16:11 reads: "You are to name him Ishmael (*which means 'God hears'*), for the LORD has heard your cry of distress." Since the original hearers and readers would have instantly understood the meaning of the name "Ishmael," we have provided modern readers with the same information so they can experience the text in a similar way.

- Many words and phrases carry a great deal of cultural meaning that was obvious to the original readers but needs explanation in our own culture. For example, the phrase "they beat their breasts" (Luke 23:48) in ancient times meant that people were very upset, often in mourning. In our translation we chose to translate this phrase dynamically for clarity: "They went home *in deep sorrow*." Then we included a footnote with the literal Greek, which reads: "Greek *went home beating their breasts.*" In other similar cases, however, we have sometimes chosen to illuminate the existing literal expression to make it immediately understandable. For example, here we might have expanded the literal Greek phrase to read: "They went home beating their breasts *in sorrow."* If we had done this, we would not have included a textual footnote, since the literal Greek clearly appears in translation.

- Metaphorical language is sometimes difficult for contemporary readers to understand, so at times we have chosen to translate or illuminate the meaning of a metaphor. For example, the ancient poet writes, "Your neck is *like* the tower of David" (Song of Songs 4:4). We have rendered it "Your neck is *as beautiful as* the tower of David" to clarify the intended positive meaning of the simile. Another example comes in Ecclesiastes 12:3, which can be literally rendered: "Remember him . . . when the grinding women cease because they are few, and the women who look through the windows see dimly." We have rendered it: "Remember him before your teeth—your few remaining servants—stop grinding; and before your eyes—the women looking through the windows—see dimly." We clarified such metaphors only when we believed a typical reader might be confused by the literal text.

- When the content of the original language text is poetic in character, we have rendered it in English poetic form. We sought to break lines in ways that clarify and highlight the relationships between phrases of the text. Hebrew poetry often uses parallelism, a literary form where a second phrase (or in some instances a third or fourth) echoes the initial phrase in some way. In Hebrew parallelism, the subsequent parallel phrases continue, while also furthering and sharpening, the thought expressed in the initial line or phrase. Whenever possible, we sought to represent these parallel phrases in natural poetic English.

- The Greek term *hoi Ioudaioi* is literally translated "the Jews" in many English translations. In the Gospel of John, however, this term doesn't always refer to the Jewish people generally. In some contexts, it refers more particularly to the Jewish religious leaders. We have attempted to capture the meaning in these different contexts by using terms such as "the people" (with a footnote: Greek *the Jewish people*) or "the religious leaders," where appropriate.

- One challenge we faced was how to translate accurately the ancient biblical text that was originally written in a context where male-oriented terms were used to refer to humanity generally. We needed to respect the nature of the ancient context while also trying to make the translation clear to a modern audience that tends to read male-oriented language as applying only to males. Often the original text, though using masculine nouns and pronouns, clearly intends that the message be applied to both men and women. A typical example is found in the New Testament letters, where the believers are called "brothers" (*adelphoi*). Yet it is clear from the content of these letters that they were addressed to all the believers—male and female. Thus, we have usually translated this Greek word as "brothers and sisters" in order to represent the historical situation more accurately.

  We have also been sensitive to passages where the text applies generally to human beings or to the human condition. In some instances we have used plural pronouns (they, them) in place of the masculine singular (he, him). For example, a traditional rendering of Proverbs 22:6 is: "Train up a child in the way he should go, and when he is old he will not turn from it." We have rendered it: "Direct your children onto the right path, and when they are older, they will not leave it." At times, we have also replaced third person pronouns with the second person to ensure clarity. A traditional rendering of Proverbs 26:27 is: "He who digs a pit will fall into it, and he who rolls a stone, it will come back on him." We have rendered it: "If you set a trap for others, you will get caught in it yourself. If you roll a boulder down on others, it will crush you instead."

  We should emphasize, however, that all masculine nouns and pronouns used to represent God (for example, "Father") have been maintained without exception. All decisions of this kind have been driven by the concern to reflect accurately the intended meaning of the original texts of Scripture.

Lexical Consistency in Terminology
For the sake of clarity, we have translated certain original-language terms consistently, especially within synoptic passages and for commonly repeated rhetorical phrases, and within

certain word categories such as divine names and non-theological technical terminology (e.g., liturgical, legal, cultural, zoological, and botanical terms). For theological terms, we have allowed a greater semantic range of acceptable English words or phrases for a single Hebrew or Greek word. We have avoided some theological terms that are not readily understood by many modern readers. For example, we avoided using words such as "justification" and "sanctification," which are carryovers from Latin translations. In place of these words, we have provided renderings such as "made right with God" and "made holy."

The Spelling of Proper Names

Many individuals in the Bible, especially the Old Testament, are known by more than one name (e.g., Uzziah/Azariah). For the sake of clarity, we have tried to use a single spelling for any one individual, footnoting the literal spelling whenever we differ from it. This is especially helpful in delineating the kings of Israel and Judah. King Joash/Jehoash of Israel has been consistently called Jehoash, while King Joash/Jehoash of Judah is called Joash. A similar distinction has been used to distinguish between Joram/Jehoram of Israel and Joram/Jehoram of Judah. All such decisions were made with the goal of clarifying the text for the reader. When the ancient biblical writers clearly had a theological purpose in their choice of a variant name (e.g., Esh-baal/Ishbosheth), the different names have been maintained with an explanatory footnote.

For the names Jacob and Israel, which are used interchangeably for both the individual patriarch and the nation, we generally render it "Israel" when it refers to the nation and "Jacob" when it refers to the individual. When our rendering of the name differs from the underlying Hebrew text, we provide a textual footnote, which includes this explanation: "The names 'Jacob' and 'Israel' are often interchanged throughout the Old Testament, referring sometimes to the individual patriarch and sometimes to the nation."

The Rendering of Divine Names

All appearances of *'el, 'elohim,* or *'eloah* have been translated "God," except where the context demands the translation "god(s)." We have generally rendered the tetragrammaton (*YHWH*) consistently as "the Lord," utilizing a form with small capitals that is common among English translations. This will distinguish it from the name *'adonai,* which we render "Lord." When *'adonai* and *YHWH* appear together, we have rendered it "Sovereign Lord." This also distinguishes *'adonai YHWH* from cases where *YHWH* appears with *'elohim,* which is rendered "Lord God." When *YH* (the short form of *YHWH*) and *YHWH* appear together, we have rendered it "Lord God." When *YHWH* appears with the term *tseba'oth,* we have rendered it "Lord of Heaven's Armies" to translate the meaning of the name. In a few cases, we have utilized the transliteration, *Yahweh,* when the personal character of the name is being invoked in contrast to another divine name or the name of some other god (for example, see Exodus 3:15; 6:2-3).

In the New Testament, the Greek word *christos* has been translated as "Messiah" when the context assumes a Jewish audience. When a Gentile audience can be assumed, *christos* has been translated as "Christ." The Greek word *kurios* is consistently translated "Lord," except that it is translated "Lord" wherever the New Testament text explicitly quotes from the Old Testament, and the text there has it in small capitals.

Textual Footnotes

The New Living Translation provides several kinds of textual footnotes, all designated in the text with an asterisk:

- When for the sake of clarity the NLT renders a difficult or potentially confusing phrase dynamically, we generally give the literal rendering in a textual footnote. This allows the reader to see the literal source of our dynamic rendering and how our translation relates to other more literal translations. These notes are prefaced with "Hebrew," "Aramaic," or "Greek," identifying the language of the underlying source text. For example, in Acts 2:42 we translated the literal "breaking of bread" (from the Greek) as "the Lord's Supper" to clarify that this verse refers to the ceremonial practice of the church rather than just an ordinary meal. Then we attached a footnote to "the Lord's Supper," which reads: "Greek *the breaking of bread.*"

- Textual footnotes are also used to show alternative renderings, prefaced with the word "Or." These normally occur for passages where an aspect of the meaning is debated. On occasion, we also provide notes on words or phrases that represent a departure from long-standing tradition. These notes are prefaced with "Tradition-ally rendered." For example, the footnote to the translation "serious skin disease" at Leviticus 13:2 says: "Traditionally rendered *leprosy.* The Hebrew word used throughout this passage is used to describe various skin diseases."

- When our translators follow a textual variant that differs significantly from our stan-dard Hebrew or Greek texts (listed earlier), we document that difference with a foot-note. We also footnote cases when the NLT excludes a passage that is included in the Greek text known as the *Textus Receptus* (and familiar to readers through its transla-tion in the King James Version). In such cases, we offer a translation of the excluded text in a footnote, even though it is generally recognized as a later addition to the Greek text and not part of the original Greek New Testament.

- All Old Testament passages that are quoted in the New Testament are identified by a textual footnote at the New Testament location. When the New Testament clearly quotes from the Greek translation of the Old Testament, and when it differs signifi-cantly in wording from the Hebrew text, we also place a textual footnote at the Old Testament location. This note includes a rendering of the Greek version, along with a cross-reference to the New Testament passage(s) where it is cited (for example, see notes on Psalms 8:2; 53:3; Proverbs 3:12).

- Some textual footnotes provide cultural and historical information on places, things, and people in the Bible that are probably obscure to modern readers. Such notes should aid the reader in understanding the message of the text. For example, in Acts 12:1, "King Herod" is named in this translation as "King Herod Agrippa" and is iden-tified in a footnote as being "the nephew of Herod Antipas and a grandson of Herod the Great."

- When the meaning of a proper name (or a wordplay inherent in a proper name) is relevant to the meaning of the text, it is either illuminated with a textual footnote or included within parentheses in the text itself. For example, the footnote concerning the name "Eve" at Genesis 3:20 reads: "*Eve* sounds like a Hebrew term that means 'to give life.' " This wordplay in the Hebrew illuminates the meaning of the text, which goes on to say that Eve "would be the mother of all who live."

AS WE SUBMIT this translation for publication, we recognize that any translation of the Scrip-tures is subject to limitations and imperfections. Anyone who has attempted to communi-cate the richness of God's Word into another language will realize it is impossible to make a perfect translation. Recognizing these limitations, we sought God's guidance and wisdom throughout this project. Now we pray that he will accept our efforts and use this translation for the benefit of the church and of all people.

We pray that the New Living Translation will overcome some of the barriers of history, cul-ture, and language that have kept people from reading and understanding God's Word. We hope that readers unfamiliar with the Bible will find the words clear and easy to understand and that readers well versed in the Scriptures will gain a fresh perspective. We pray that readers will gain insight and wisdom for living, but most of all that they will meet the God of the Bible and be forever changed by knowing him.

The Bible Translation Committee
October 2007

WHY THE
LIFE APPLICATION STUDY BIBLE
IS UNIQUE

Have you ever opened your Bible and asked the following:

- What does this passage really mean?
- How does it apply to my life?
- Why does some of the Bible seem irrelevant?
- What do these ancient cultures have to do with today?
- I love God; why can't I understand what he is saying to me through his word?
- What's going on in the lives of these Bible people?

Many Christians do not read the Bible regularly. Why? Because in the pressures of daily living they cannot find a connection between the timeless principles of Scripture and the ever-present problems of day-by-day living.

God urges us to apply his word (Isaiah 42:23; 1 Corinthians 10:11; 2 Thessalonians 3:4), but too often we stop at accumulating Bible knowledge. This is why the *Life Application Study Bible* was developed—to show how to put into practice what we have learned.

Applying God's word is a vital part of one's relationship with God; it is the evidence that we are obeying him. The difficulty in applying the Bible is not with the Bible itself, but with the reader's inability to bridge the gap between the past and present, the conceptual and practical. When we don't or can't do this, spiritual dryness, shallowness, and indifference are the results.

The words of Scripture itself cry out to us, "But don't just listen to God's word. You must do what it says. Otherwise, you are only fooling yourselves" (James 1:22). The *Life Application Study Bible* helps us to obey God's word. Developed by an interdenominational team of pastors, scholars, family counselors, and a national organization dedicated to promoting God's word and spreading the gospel, the *Life Application Study Bible* took many years to complete. All the work was reviewed by several renowned theologians under the directorship of Dr. Kenneth Kantzer.

The Life Application Study Bible does what a good resource Bible should: It helps you understand the context of a passage, gives important background and historical information, explains difficult words and phrases, and helps you see the interrelationship of Scripture. But it does much more. The *Life Application Study Bible* goes deeper into God's word, helping you discover the timeless truth being communicated, see the relevance for your life, and make a personal application. While some study Bibles attempt application, over 75 percent of this Bible is application oriented. The notes answer the questions "So what?" and "What does this passage mean to me, my family, my friends, my job, my neighborhood, my church, my country?"

Imagine reading a familiar passage of Scripture and gaining fresh insight, as if it were the first time you had ever read it. How much richer your life would be if you left each Bible reading with a new perspective and a small change for the better. A small change every day adds up to a changed life—and that is the very purpose of Scripture.

WHAT IS APPLICATION?

The best way to define application is to first determine what it is *not*. Application is *not* just accumulating knowledge. Accumulating knowledge helps us discover and understand facts and concepts, but it stops there. History is filled with philosophers who knew what the Bible said but failed to apply it to their lives, keeping them from believing and changing. Many think that understanding is the end goal of Bible study, but it is really only the beginning.

Application is *not* just illustration. Illustration only tells us how someone else handled a similar situation. While we may empathize with that person, we still have little direction for our personal situation.

Application is *not* just making a passage "relevant." Making the Bible relevant only helps us to see that the same lessons that were true in Bible times are true today; it does not show us how to apply them to the problems and pressures of our individual lives.

What, then, is application? Application begins by knowing and understanding God's word and its timeless truths. *But you cannot stop there.* If you do, God's word may not change your life, and it may become dull, difficult, tedious, and tiring. A good application focuses the truth of God's word, shows the reader what to do about what is being read, and motivates the reader to respond to what God is teaching. All three are essential to application.

Application is putting into practice what we already know (see Mark 4:24 and Hebrews 5:14) and answering the question "So what?" by confronting us with the right questions and motivating us to take action (see 1 John 2:5-6 and James 2:26). Application is deeply personal—unique for each individual. It makes a relevant truth a personal truth and involves developing a strategy and action plan to live your life in harmony with the Bible. It is the biblical "how to" of life.

You may ask, "How can your application notes be relevant to my life?" Each application note has three parts: (1) an *explanation*, which ties the note directly to the Scripture passage and sets up the truth that is being taught; (2) the *bridge*, which explains the timeless truth and makes it relevant for today; (3) the *application*, which shows you how to take the timeless truth and apply it to your personal situation. No note, by itself, can apply Scripture directly to your life. It can only teach, direct, lead, guide, inspire, recommend, and urge. It can give you the resources and direction you need to apply the Bible, but only you can take these resources and put them into practice.

A good note, therefore should not only give you knowledge and understanding but point you to application. Before you buy any kind of resource study Bible, you should evaluate the notes and ask the following questions: (1) Does the note contain enough information to help me understand the point of the Scripture passage? (2) Does the note assume I know more than I do? (3) Does the note avoid denominational bias? (4) Do the notes touch most of life's experiences? (5) Does the note help me apply God's word?

FEATURES OF THE
LIFE APPLICATION STUDY BIBLE

NOTES
In addition to providing the reader with many application notes, the *Life Application Study Bible* offers explanatory notes that help the reader understand culture, history, context, difficult-to-understand passages, background, places, theological concepts, and the relationship of various passages in Scripture to other passages.

BOOK INTRODUCTIONS
Each book introduction is divided into several easy-to-find parts:

Timeline. A guide that puts the Bible book into its historical setting. It lists the key events and the dates when they occurred.

Vital Statistics. A list of straight facts about the book—those pieces of information you need to know at a glance.

Overview. A summary of the book with general lessons and applications that can be learned from the book as a whole.

Blueprint. The outline of the book. It is printed in easy-to-understand language and is designed for easy memorization. To the right of each mean heading is a key lesson that is taught in that particular section.

Megathemes. A section that gives the main themes of the Bible book, explains their significance, and then tells you why they are still important for us today.

Map. If included, this shows the key places found in that book and retells the story of the book from a geographical perspective.

OUTLINE
The *Life Application Study Bible* has a new, custom-made outline that was designed specifically from an application point of view. Several unique features should be noted:

1. To avoid confusion and to aid memory work, the book outline has only three levels for headings. Main outline heads are marked with a capital letter. Subheads are marked by a number. Minor explanatory heads have no letter or number.

2. Each main outline head marked by a letter also has a brief paragraph below it summarizing the Bible text and offering a general application.

3. Parallel passages are listed where they apply.

PROFILE NOTES
Among the unique features of this Bible are the profiles of key Bible people, including their strengths and weaknesses, greatest accomplishments and mistakes, and key lessons from their lives.

MAPS
The *Life Application Study Bible* has a thorough and comprehensive Bible atlas built right into the book. There are two kinds of maps: a book-introduction map, telling the story of the book, and thumbnail maps in the notes, plotting most geographic movements.

CHARTS AND DIAGRAMS
Many charts and diagrams are included to help the reader better visualize difficult concepts or relationships. Most charts not only present the needed information but show the significance of the information as well.

CROSS-REFERENCES
An updated, exhaustive cross-reference system in the margins of the Bible text helps the reader find related passages quickly.

TEXTUAL NOTES
Directly related to the text of the New Living Translation, the textual notes provide explanations on certain wording in the translation, alternate translations, and information about readings in the ancient manuscripts.

HIGHLIGHTED NOTES
In each Bible study lesson, you will be asked to read specific notes as part of your preparation. These notes have each been highlighted by a bullet (•) so that you can find them easily.

JAMES

JAMES

"MIRACULOUS!" . . . "Revolutionary!" . . . "Greatest ever!" We are inundated by a flood of extravagant claims as we channel surf the television or flip magazine pages. The messages leap out at us. The products assure that they are new, improved, fantastic, and capable of changing our lives. For only a few dollars, we can have "cleaner clothes," "whiter teeth," "glamorous hair," and "tastier food." Automobiles, perfume, diet drinks, and mouthwash are guaranteed to bring happiness, friends, and the good life. And just before an election, no one can match the politicians' promises. But talk is cheap, and too often we soon realize that the boasts were hollow, quite far from the truth.

"Jesus is the answer!" . . . "Believe in God!" . . . "Follow me to church!" Christians also make great claims but are often guilty of belying them with their actions. Professing to trust God and to be his people, they cling tightly to the world and its values. Possessing all the right answers, they contradict the gospel with their lives.

With energetic style and crisp, well-chosen words, James confronts this conflict head-on. It is not enough to talk the Christian faith, he says; we must live it. "What good is it, dear brothers and sisters, if you say you have faith but don't show it by your actions? Can that kind of faith save anyone?" (2:14). The proof of the reality of our faith is a changed life.

Genuine faith will inevitably produce good deeds. This is the central theme of James' letter, around which he supplies practical advice on living the Christian life.

James begins his letter by outlining some general characteristics of the Christian life (1:1–27). Next, he exhorts Christians to act justly in society (2:1–13). He follows this practical advice with a theological discourse on the relationship between faith and action (2:14–26). Then James shows the importance of controlling one's speech (3:1–12). In 3:13–18, James distinguishes two kinds of wisdom—earthly and heavenly. Then he encourages his readers to turn from evil desires and obey God (4:1–12). James reproves those who trust in their own plans and possessions (4:13—5:6). Finally, he exhorts his readers to be patient with each other (5:7–11), to be straightforward in their promises (5:12), to pray for each other (5:13–18), and to help each other remain faithful to God (5:19, 20).

This letter could be considered a how-to book on Christian living. Confrontation, challenges, and a call to commitment await you in its pages. Read James and become a *doer* of the Word (1:22–25).

VITAL STATISTICS

PURPOSE:
To expose hypocritical practices and to teach right Christian behavior

AUTHOR:
James, Jesus' brother, a leader in the Jerusalem church

ORIGINAL AUDIENCE:
First-century Jewish Christians residing in Gentile communities outside Palestine

DATE WRITTEN:
Probably A.D. 49, prior to the Jerusalem council held in A.D. 50

SETTING:
This letter expresses James' concern for persecuted Christians who were once part of the Jerusalem church.

KEY VERSE:
"Now someone may argue, 'Some people have faith; others have good deeds.' But I say, 'How can you show me your faith if you don't have good deeds? I will show you my faith by my good deeds'" (2:18).

THE BLUEPRINT

1. Genuine religion (1:1–27)
2. Genuine faith (2:1—3:12)
3. Genuine wisdom (3:13—5:20)

James wrote to Jewish Christians who had been scattered throughout the Mediterranean world because of persecution. In their hostile surroundings they were tempted to let intellectual agreement pass for true faith. This letter can have rich meaning for us as we are reminded that genuine faith transforms lives. We are encouraged to put our faith into action. It is easy to say we have faith, but true faith will produce loving actions toward others.

MEGATHEMES

THEME	EXPLANATION	IMPORTANCE
Living Faith	James wants believers not only to hear the truth but also to put it into action. He contrasts empty faith (claims without conduct) with faith that works. Commitment to love and to serve others is evidence of true faith.	Living faith makes a difference. Make sure your faith is more than just a statement; it should also result in action. Seek ways of putting your faith to work.
Trials	In the Christian life there are trials and temptations. Successfully overcoming these adversities produces maturity and strong character.	Don't resent troubles when they come. Pray for wisdom; God will supply all you need to face persecution or adversity. He will give you patience and keep you strong in times of trial.
Law of Love	We are saved by God's gracious mercy, not by keeping the law. But Christ gave us a special command: "Love your neighbor as yourself" (Matthew 19:19). We are to love and serve those around us.	Keeping the law of love shows that our faith is vital and real. When we show love to others, we are overcoming our own selfishness.
Wise Speech	Wisdom shows itself in wise speech. God holds us responsible for the results of our destructive words. The wisdom of God that helps control the tongue can help control all our actions.	Accepting God's wisdom will affect your speech. Your words will convey true humility and lead to peace. Think before you speak and allow God to give you self-control.
Wealth	James taught Christians not to compromise with worldly attitudes about wealth. Because the glory of wealth fades, Christians should store up God's treasures through sincere service. Christians must not show partiality to the wealthy or be prejudiced against the poor.	All of us are accountable for how we use what we have. We should not hoard wealth but be generous toward others. In addition, we should not be impressed by the wealthy nor look down on those who are poor.

1. Genuine religion

Greetings from James

1 This letter is from James, a slave of God and of the Lord Jesus Christ. I am writing to the "twelve tribes"—Jewish believers scattered abroad. Greetings!

1:1
1 Pet 1:1

Faith and Endurance

²Dear brothers and sisters,* when troubles come your way, consider it an opportunity for great joy. ³For you know that when your faith is tested, your endurance has a chance to grow. ⁴So let it grow, for when your endurance is fully developed, you will be perfect and complete, needing nothing.

⁵If you need wisdom, ask our generous God, and he will give it to you. He will not rebuke

1:2
1 Pet 1:6
1:3
1 Pet 1:7
1:5
Prov 2:3-6
Matt 7:7

1:2 Greek *brothers;* also in 1:16, 19.

• **1:1** The writer of this letter, a leader of the church in Jerusalem (see Acts 12:17; 15:13), was James, Jesus' half brother, not James the apostle. The book of James was one of the earliest letters, probably written before A.D. 50. After Stephen was martyred (Acts 7:55–8:3), persecution increased, and Christians in Jerusalem were scattered throughout the Roman world. There were thriving Jewish-Christian communities in Rome, Alexandria, Cyprus, and cities in Greece and Asia Minor. Because these early believers did not have the support of established Christian churches, James wrote to them as a concerned leader, to encourage them in their faith during those difficult times.

• **1:2, 3** James doesn't say *if* trouble comes your way but *when* it does. He assumes that we will have troubles and that it is possible to profit from them. The point is not to pretend to be happy when we face pain but to have a positive outlook ("consider it an opportunity for great joy") because of what troubles can produce in our life. James tells us to turn our hardships into times of learning. Tough times can teach us perseverance. For other passages dealing with perseverance (also called patience and steadfastness), see Romans 2:7; 5:3-5; 8:24, 25; 2 Corinthians 6:3-7; 2 Peter 1:2-9.

• **1:2-4** We can't really know the depth of our character until we see how we react under pressure. It is easy to be kind to others when everything is going well, but can we still be kind when others are treating us unfairly? God wants to make us mature and complete, not to keep us from all pain. Instead of complaining about our struggles, we should see them as opportunities for growth. Thank God for promising to be with you in rough times. Ask him to help you solve your problems or to give you the strength to endure them. Then be patient. God will not leave you alone with your problems; he will stay close and help you grow.

• **1:5** By "wisdom," James is talking not only about knowledge but about the ability to make wise decisions in difficult circumstances. Whenever we need wisdom, we can pray to God, and he will generously supply what we need. Christians don't have to grope around in the dark, hoping to stumble upon answers. We can ask for God's wisdom to guide our choices.

• **1:5** The wisdom that we need has three distinct characteristics:

(1) *It is practical.* The wisdom from God relates to life even during the most trying times. It is not a wisdom isolated from suffering and trials. This wisdom is the tool by which trials are overcome. An intelligent person may have profound ideas, but a wise person puts profound ideas into action. Intelligence will allow someone to describe several reasons why the car broke down. The wise person chooses the most likely reason and proceeds to take action.

(2) *It is divine.* God's wisdom goes beyond common sense.

1:6
Matt 21:22
Mark 11:24

you for asking. 6 But when you ask him, be sure that your faith is in God alone. Do not waver, for a person with divided loyalty is as unsettled as a wave of the sea that is blown and tossed by the wind. 7 Such people should not expect to receive anything from the Lord. 8 Their loyalty is divided between God and the world, and they are unstable in everything they do.

1:10-11
Ps 102:4, 11
Isa 40:6-7
1 Pet 1:24

9 Believers who are* poor have something to boast about, for God has honored them. 10 And those who are rich should boast that God has humbled them. They will fade away like a little flower in the field. 11 The hot sun rises and the grass withers; the little flower droops and falls, and its beauty fades away. In the same way, the rich will fade away with all of their achievements.

1:12
1 Cor 9:25
2 Tim 4:8
Jas 5:11
Rev 2:10; 3:11

12 God blesses those who patiently endure testing and temptation. Afterward they will receive the crown of life that God has promised to those who love him. 13 And remember,

1:9 Greek *The brother who is.*

CHAPTER SUMMARY

Chapter 1 . . . . Confident Stand . . . . What a Christian has
Chapter 2 . . . . Compassionate Service . . . . What a Christian does
Chapter 3 . . . . Careful Speech . . . . What a Christian says
Chapter 4 . . . . Contrite Submission . . . . What a Christian feels
Chapter 5 . . . . Concerned Sharing . . . . What a Christian gives

Common sense does not lead us to choose joy in the middle of trials. This wisdom begins with respect for God, leads to living by God's direction, and results in the ability to tell right from wrong. It is a wisdom that James will describe at length in chapter 3.

(3) *It is Christlike.* Asking for wisdom is ultimately asking to be like Christ. The Bible identifies Christ as the "wisdom of God" (1 Corinthians 1:24; 2:1-7).

• **1:6** We must believe not only in the existence of God but also in his loving care. This includes relying on God and expecting that he will hear and answer when we pray. We must put away our critical attitude when we come to him. God does not grant every thoughtless or selfish request. We must have confidence that God will align our desires with his purposes. For more on this concept, read the note on Matthew 21:22.

• **1:6** A person with divided loyalty is not completely convinced that God's way is best. He treats God's Word like any human advice and retains the option to disobey. He vacillates between allegiance to subjective feelings, the world's ideas, and God's commands. If your faith is new, weak, or struggling, remember that you can trust God. Then be loyal by committing yourself wholeheartedly to God.

• **1:6-8** If you have ever seen the constant rolling of huge waves at sea, you know how restless they are—subject to the forces of wind, gravity, and tide. Divided loyalty leaves a person as unsettled as the restless waves. If you want to stop being tossed about, rely on God to show you what is best for you. Ask him for wisdom, and trust that he will give it to you. Then your decisions will be sure and solid.

1:9 Christianity brings a new dignity to the poor and not-so-influential people of this world. That dignity is most apparent in the church, where there are not (or should not be) any class distinctions. All believers share the distinction and dignity of being changed by the gospel and being charged with the mission of taking that same Good News to the rest of the world. Believers know they have dignity before God because Christ died for them. Mary, the mother of Jesus, is a great example of this truth. The dignity that she displayed when she realized what God had done for her is seen in her prayer of praise, called the *Magnificat* (Luke 1:46-55). Whatever our social or economic situation, James challenges us to see beyond it to our eternal advantages. What we can have in Jesus Christ outweighs anything in this life. Knowing him gives us our high position, where we find our true dignity.

1:9-11 The poor should be glad that riches mean nothing to God; otherwise these people would be considered unworthy. The rich

should be glad that money means nothing to God because money is easily lost. We find true wealth by developing our spiritual life, not by developing our financial assets. God is interested in what is lasting (our souls), not in what is temporary (our money and possessions). See Mark 4:18, 19 for Jesus' words on this subject. Strive to treat each person as Christ would treat him or her.

1:10, 11 If wealth, power, and status mean nothing to God, why do we attribute so much importance to them and so much honor to those who possess them? Do your material possessions give you goals and your only reason for living? If they were gone, what would be left? What you have in your heart, not your bank account, matters to God and endures for eternity.

• **1:12** The crown of life is like the victory wreath given to winning athletes (see 1 Corinthians 9:25). God's crown of life is not glory and honor here on earth but the reward of eternal life—living with God forever. The way to be in God's winners' circle is by loving him and staying faithful even under pressure.

• **1:12-15** Temptation comes from evil desires inside us, not from God. It begins with an evil thought and becomes sin when we dwell on the thought and allow it to become an action. Like a snowball rolling downhill, sin grows more destructive the more we let it have its way. The best time to stop a temptation is before it is too strong or moving too fast to control. See Matthew 4:1-11; 1 Corinthians 10:13; and 2 Timothy 2:22 for more about escaping temptation.

• **1:13, 14** People who live for God often wonder why they still have temptations. Does God tempt them? God *tests* people, but he does not *tempt* them by trying to seduce them to sin. God allows Satan to tempt people, however, in order to refine their faith and to help them grow in their dependence on Christ. We can resist the temptation to sin by turning to God for strength and choosing to obey his Word.

• **1:13-15** It is easy to blame others and make excuses for evil thoughts and wrong actions. We use excuses such as: (1) It's the other person's fault; (2) I couldn't help it; (3) everybody's doing it; (4) it was just a mistake; (5) nobody's perfect; (6) the devil made me do it; (7) I was pressured into it; (8) I didn't know it was wrong; or (9) God is tempting me. A person who makes excuses is trying to shift the blame from himself or herself to something or someone else. A Christian, on the other hand, accepts responsibility for his or her wrongs, confesses them, and asks God for forgiveness.

when you are being tempted, do not say, "God is tempting me." God is never tempted to do wrong,* and he never tempts anyone else. ¹⁴Temptation comes from our own desires, which entice us and drag us away. ¹⁵These desires give birth to sinful actions. And when sin is allowed to grow, it gives birth to death.

¹⁶So don't be misled, my dear brothers and sisters. ¹⁷Whatever is good and perfect comes down to us from God our Father, who created all the lights in the heavens.* He never changes or casts a shifting shadow.* ¹⁸He chose to give birth to us by giving us his true word. And we, out of all creation, became his prized possession.*

Listening and Doing

¹⁹Understand this, my dear brothers and sisters: You must all be quick to listen, slow to speak, and slow to get angry. ²⁰Human anger* does not produce the righteousness* God desires. ²¹So get rid of all the filth and evil in your lives, and humbly accept the word God has planted in your hearts, for it has the power to save your souls.

²²But don't just listen to God's word. You must do what it says. Otherwise, you are only fooling yourselves. ²³For if you listen to the word and don't obey, it is like glancing at your face in a mirror. ²⁴You see yourself, walk away, and forget what you look like. ²⁵But if you look carefully into the perfect law that sets you free, and if you do what it says and don't forget what you heard, then God will bless you for doing it.

²⁶If you claim to be religious but don't control your tongue, you are fooling yourself, and your religion is worthless. ²⁷Pure and genuine religion in the sight of God the Father means caring for orphans and widows in their distress and refusing to let the world corrupt you.

2. Genuine faith

A Warning against Prejudice

2 My dear brothers and sisters,* how can you claim to have faith in our glorious Lord Jesus Christ if you favor some people over others?

1:14 Prov 19:3
1:16 1 Cor 6:9
1:17 Gen 1:16 / Ps 136:7 / Matt 7:11
1:18 John 1:13 / 1 Pet 1:23
1:19 Prov 10:19; 15:1 / Eccl 7:9
1:21 Eph 1:13; 4:22 / 1 Pet 2:1
1:22 Matt 7:21, 26 / Rom 2:13
1:25 John 13:17 / Rom 8:2 / Gal 6:2 / Jas 2:12 / 1 Pet 2:16
1:26 Ps 34:13
1:27 Deut 14:29 / 1 Jn 2:15-17
2:1 Prov 24:23 / Acts 10:34 / 1 Cor 2:8

1:13 Or *God should not be put to a test by evil people.* **1:17a** Greek *from above, from the Father of lights.* **1:17b** Some manuscripts read *He never changes, as a shifting shadow does.* **1:18** Greek *we became a kind of firstfruit of his creatures.* **1:20a** Greek *A man's anger.* **1:20b** Or *the justice.* **2:1** Greek *brothers;* also in 2:5, 14.

1:17 The Bible often compares goodness with light and evil with shadow and darkness. For other passages where God is pictured as light, see Psalm 27:1, Isaiah 60:19-22, and John 1:1-14.

• **1:19** When we talk too much and listen too little, we communicate to others that we think our ideas are more important than theirs. James wisely advises us to reverse this process. Put a mental stopwatch on your conversations, and keep track of how much you talk and how much you listen. When people talk with you, do they feel that their viewpoints and ideas have value?

• **1:19, 20** These verses speak of anger that erupts when our ego is bruised: *"I* am hurt;" *"My* opinions are not being heard." When injustice and sin occur, we *should* become angry because others are being hurt. But we should not become angry when we fail to win an argument or when we feel offended or neglected. Selfish anger never helps anybody.

1:21 James advises us to get rid of all that is wrong in our lives and "humbly accept" the salvation message we have received, because it alone can save us.

• **1:22-25** It is important to listen to what God's Word says, but it is much more important to obey it and to *do* what it says. We can measure the effectiveness of our Bible study time by the effect it has on our behavior and attitudes. Do you put into action what you have studied?

• **1:25** It seems paradoxical that a law could give us freedom, but God's law offers us a true reflection of our sinful condition and gives us the opportunity to ask for God's forgiveness (see Romans 7:7, 8). As Christians, we are saved by God's grace, and salvation frees us from sin's control. As believers, we are free to live as God created us to live. Of course, this does not mean that we are free to do as we please (see 1 Peter 2:16). We are now free to obey God.

1:26 See the notes in chapter 3 for more on controlling the tongue. No matter how spiritual we may think we are, we all could control our speech more effectively.

• **1:27** In the first century, orphans and widows had very little means of economic support. Unless a family member was willing to care for them, they were reduced to begging, selling themselves as slaves, or starving. By caring for these people, the church put God's Word into practice. When we give with no thought of receiving, we show what it means to truly serve others.

• **1:27** To keep ourselves from letting the world corrupt us, we need to commit ourselves to Christ's ethical and moral system, not the world's. We are not to adapt to the world's value system, which is based on money, power, and pleasure. True faith means nothing if we are contaminated with such values.

• **2:1ff** In this chapter James argues against favoritism and for the necessity of good deeds. He presents three principles of faith: (1) Commitment is an essential part of faith. You cannot be a Christian simply by affirming the right doctrines or agreeing with biblical facts (2:19). You must commit your mind and heart to Christ. (2) Right actions are the natural by-products of true faith. A genuine Christian will have a changed life (2:18). (3) Faith without good deeds doesn't do anybody any good—it is useless (2:14-17). James's teachings are consistent with Paul's teaching that we receive salvation by faith alone. Paul emphasizes the purpose of faith: to bring salvation. James emphasizes the results of faith: a changed life.

• **2:1-7** James condemns acts of favoritism. Often we treat a well-dressed, impressive-looking person better than someone who looks shabby. We do this because we would rather identify with successful people than with apparent failures. The irony, as James reminds us, is that the supposed winners may have gained their impressive lifestyle at our expense. In addition, the rich find it difficult to identify with the Lord Jesus, who came as a humble servant. Are you easily impressed by status, wealth, or fame? Are you partial to the "haves" while ignoring the "have nots"? This attitude is sinful. God views all people as equals, and if he favors anyone, it is the poor and the powerless. We should follow his example.

²For example, suppose someone comes into your meeting* dressed in fancy clothes and expensive jewelry, and another comes in who is poor and dressed in dirty clothes. ³If you give special attention and a good seat to the rich person, but you say to the poor one, "You can stand over there, or else sit on the floor"—well, ⁴doesn't this discrimination show that your judgments are guided by evil motives?

⁵Listen to me, dear brothers and sisters. Hasn't God chosen the poor in this world to be rich in faith? Aren't they the ones who will inherit the Kingdom he promised to those who love him? ⁶But you dishonor the poor! Isn't it the rich who oppress you and drag you into court? ⁷Aren't they the ones who slander Jesus Christ, whose noble name* you bear?

⁸Yes indeed, it is good when you obey the royal law as found in the Scriptures: "Love your neighbor as yourself."* ⁹But if you favor some people over others, you are committing a sin. You are guilty of breaking the law.

¹⁰For the person who keeps all of the laws except one is as guilty as a person who has broken all of God's laws. ¹¹For the same God who said, "You must not commit adultery," also said, "You must not murder."* So if you murder someone but do not commit adultery, you have still broken the law.

¹²So whatever you say or whatever you do, remember that you will be judged by the law

2:4
John 7:23-24

2:5
Luke 6:20
1 Cor 1:26-28

2:7
Acts 11:26
1 Pet 4:16

2:8
†Lev 19:18
Matt 7:12
Rom 13:8

2:10
Matt 5:19
Gal 5:3

2:11
†Exod 20:13-14
†Deut 5:17-18
Matt 19:18

2:12
Jas 1:25

2:2 Greek *your synagogue.*   **2:7** Greek *slander the noble name.*   **2:8** Lev 19:18.   **2:11** Exod 20:13-14; Deut 5:17-18.

SHOWING FAVORITISM
Why it is wrong to show favoritism to the wealthy:

1. It is inconsistent with Christ's teachings.
2. It results from evil thoughts.
3. It insults people made in God's image.
4. It is a by-product of selfish motives.
5. It goes against the biblical definition of love.
6. It shows a lack of mercy to those less fortunate.
7. It is hypocritical.
8. It is a sin.

• **2:2-4** Why is it wrong to judge a person by his or her economic status? Wealth may indicate intelligence, wise decisions, and hard work. On the other hand, it may only mean that a person had the good fortune of being born into a wealthy family. Or it may be the sign of greed, dishonesty, or selfishness. By honoring someone just because he or she dresses well, we are making appearance more important than character. Sometimes we do this because: (1) poverty makes us uncomfortable; we don't want to face our responsibilities to those who have less than we do; (2) we want to be wealthy, too, and hope to use the rich person as a means to that end; (3) we want the rich person to join our church and help support it financially. All these motives are selfish, stemming from the view that we are superior to the poor person. If we say that Christ is our Lord, then we must live as he requires, showing no favoritism and loving all people regardless of whether they are rich or poor.

2:2-4 We are often partial to the rich because we mistakenly assume that riches are a sign of God's blessing and approval. But God does not promise us earthly rewards or riches; in fact, Christ calls us to be ready to suffer for him and give up everything in order to hold on to eternal life (Matthew 6:19-21; 19:28-30; Luke 12:14-34; Romans 8:15-21; 1 Timothy 6:17-19). We will have untold riches in eternity if we are faithful in our present life (Luke 6:35; John 12:23-25; Galatians 6:7-10; Titus 3:4-8).

• **2:5** When James speaks about the poor, he is talking about those who have no money and also about those whose simple values are despised by much of our affluent society. Perhaps the "poor" people prefer serving to managing, human relationships to financial security, peace to power. This does not mean that the poor will automatically go to heaven and the rich to hell. Poor people, however, are usually more aware of their powerlessness. Thus, it is often easier for them to acknowledge their need for

salvation. One of the greatest barriers to salvation for the rich is pride. For the poor, bitterness can often bar the way to acceptance of salvation.

2:8 The "royal law" was given by our great King Jesus Christ, who said, "Love each other in the same way that I have loved you" (John 15:12). This law, originally summarized in Leviticus 19:18, is the basis for all the laws of how people should relate to one another. Christ reinforced this truth in Matthew 22:37-40, and Paul taught it in Romans 13:8 and Galatians 5:14.

• **2:8, 9** We must treat all people as we would want to be treated. We should not ignore the rich, because then we would be withholding our love. But we must not favor them for what they can do for us, while ignoring the poor who can offer us seemingly so little in return.

2:10 Christians must not use this verse to justify sinning. We dare not say, "Because I can't keep every demand of God, why even try?" James reminds us that if we've broken just one law, we are sinners. We can't decide to keep part of God's law and ignore the rest. You can't break the law a little bit; if you have broken it at all, you need Christ to pay for your sin. Measure yourself, not someone else, against God's standards. Ask for forgiveness where you need it, and then renew your effort to put your faith into practice.

• **2:12** As Christians, we are saved by God's free gift (grace) through faith, not by keeping the law. But as Christians, we are also required to obey Christ. The apostle Paul taught that "we must all stand before Christ to be judged" (2 Corinthians 5:10) for our conduct. God's grace does not cancel our duty to obey him; it gives our obedience a new basis. The law is no longer an external set of rules, but it is a "law that sets you free"—one we joyfully and willingly carry out, because we love God and have the power of his Holy Spirit (see 1:25).

that sets you free. ¹³There will be no mercy for those who have not shown mercy to others. But if you have been merciful, God will be merciful when he judges you.

Faith without Good Deeds Is Dead

¹⁴What good is it, dear brothers and sisters, if you say you have faith but don't show it by your actions? Can that kind of faith save anyone? ¹⁵Suppose you see a brother or sister who has no food or clothing, ¹⁶and you say, "Good-bye and have a good day; stay warm and eat well"—but then you don't give that person any food or clothing. What good does that do?

¹⁷So you see, faith by itself isn't enough. Unless it produces good deeds, it is dead and useless.

¹⁸Now someone may argue, "Some people have faith; others have good deeds." But I say, "How can you show me your faith if you don't have good deeds? I will show you my faith by my good deeds."

¹⁹You say you have faith, for you believe that there is one God.* Good for you! Even the demons believe this, and they tremble in terror. ²⁰How foolish! Can't you see that faith without good deeds is useless?

²¹Don't you remember that our ancestor Abraham was shown to be right with God by his actions when he offered his son Isaac on the altar? ²²You see, his faith and his actions worked together. His actions made his faith complete. ²³And so it happened just as the Scriptures say: "Abraham believed God, and God counted him as righteous because of his faith."* He was even called the friend of God.* ²⁴So you see, we are shown to be right with God by what we do, not by faith alone.

²⁵Rahab the prostitute is another example. She was shown to be right with God by her actions when she hid those messengers and sent them safely away by a different road. ²⁶Just as the body is dead without breath,* so also faith is dead without good works.

Controlling the Tongue

3 Dear brothers and sisters,* not many of you should become teachers in the church, for we who teach will be judged more strictly. ²Indeed, we all make many mistakes. For if we could control our tongues, we would be perfect and could also control ourselves in every other way.

³We can make a large horse go wherever we want by means of a small bit in its mouth. ⁴And a small rudder makes a huge ship turn wherever the pilot chooses to go, even though the winds are strong. ⁵In the same way, the tongue is a small thing that makes grand speeches.

Cross references (right margin):
- **2:13** Matt 18:32-35
- **2:15** Matt 25:35-36
- **2:16** 1 Jn 3:17-18
- **2:17** Gal 5:6; Jas 2:20, 26
- **2:18** Matt 7:16-17; Rom 3:28
- **2:19** Deut 6:4; Matt 8:29
- **2:20** Gal 5:6; Jas 2:14, 17, 26
- **2:21** Gen 22:9, 12
- **2:22** Heb 11:17
- **2:23** †Gen 15:6; Isa 41:8; Rom 4:3-5
- **2:25** Josh 2:4, 6, 15; Heb 11:31
- **2:26** Gal 5:6; Jas 2:14, 17, 20
- **3:1** Rom 2:21
- **3:2** Jas 1:4, 26
- **3:3** Ps 32:9
- **3:5** Prov 26:20

2:19 Some manuscripts read *that God is one;* see Deut 6:4.   **2:23a** Gen 15:6.   **2:23b** See Isa 41:8.
2:26 Or *without spirit.*   **3:1** Greek *brothers;* also in 3:10.

- **2:13** Only God in his mercy can forgive our sins. We can't earn forgiveness by forgiving others. But when we withhold forgiveness from others after having received it ourselves, we show that we don't understand or appreciate God's mercy toward us (see Matthew 6:14, 15; 18:21ff; Ephesians 4:31, 32).

- **2:14** When someone claims to have faith, what he or she may have is intellectual assent—agreement with a set of Christian teachings—and as such it would be incomplete faith. True faith transforms our conduct as well as our thoughts. If our life remains unchanged, we don't truly believe the truths we claim to believe.

- **2:17** We cannot earn our salvation by serving and obeying God. But such actions show that our commitment to God is real. Deeds of loving service are not a substitute for, but rather a verification of, our faith in Christ.

- **2:18** At first glance, this verse seems to contradict Romans 3:28, "We are made right with God through faith and not by obeying the law." Deeper investigation, however, shows that the teachings of James and Paul are not at odds. While it is true that our good deeds can never earn salvation, true faith always results in a changed life and good deeds. Paul speaks against those who try to be saved by deeds instead of true faith; James speaks against those who confuse mere intellectual assent with true faith. After all, even demons know who Jesus is, but they don't obey him (2:19). True faith involves a commitment of your whole self to God.

- **2:21-24** James says that Abraham was "shown to be right with God" for what he *did* because he *believed* God (Romans 4:1-5). James and Paul are not contradicting but complementing each other. Let's not conclude that the truth is a blending of these two statements. We are not justified by what we do in any way. True faith always results in good deeds, but the deeds do not justify us. Faith brings us salvation; active obedience demonstrates that our faith is genuine.

- **2:25** Rahab lived in Jericho, a city the Israelites conquered as they entered the Promised Land (Joshua 2). When Israel's spies came to the city, she hid them and helped them escape. In this way she demonstrated faith in God's purpose for Israel. As a result, she and her family were saved when the city was destroyed. Hebrews 11:31 lists Rahab among the heroes of faith.

3:1 Teaching was a highly valued and respected profession in Jewish culture, and many Jews who embraced Christianity wanted to become teachers. James warned that although it is good to aspire to teach, teachers' responsibility is great because their words and example affect others' spiritual lives. If you are in a teaching or leadership role, how are you affecting those you lead?

- **3:2, 3** What you say and what you *don't* say are both important. To use proper speech you must not only say the right words at the right time but also not say what you shouldn't. Examples of an untamed tongue include gossiping, putting others down, bragging, manipulating, false teaching, exaggerating, complaining, flattering, and lying. Before you speak, ask, Is what I want to say true? Is it necessary? Is it kind?

3:6
Prov 16:27
Matt 12:36-37;
15:11, 18-19

3:8
Ps 140:3
Rom 3:13

3:9
Gen 1:26-27; 5:1
1 Cor 11:7

3:12
Matt 7:16

But a tiny spark can set a great forest on fire. 6And the tongue is a flame of fire. It is a whole world of wickedness, corrupting your entire body. It can set your whole life on fire, for it is set on fire by hell itself.*

7People can tame all kinds of animals, birds, reptiles, and fish, 8but no one can tame the tongue. It is restless and evil, full of deadly poison. 9Sometimes it praises our Lord and Father, and sometimes it curses those who have been made in the image of God. 10And so blessing and cursing come pouring out of the same mouth. Surely, my brothers and sisters, this is not right! 11Does a spring of water bubble out with both fresh water and bitter water? 12Does a fig tree produce olives, or a grapevine produce figs? No, and you can't draw fresh water from a salty spring.*

3. Genuine wisdom
True Wisdom Comes from God

3:13
Jas 2:18

3:14
2 Cor 12:20

3:15
Jas 1:5, 17

3:16
1 Cor 3:3
Gal 5:20-21

3:17
Rom 12:9
Heb 12:11

3:18
Matt 5:9
Phil 1:11

13If you are wise and understand God's ways, prove it by living an honorable life, doing good works with the humility that comes from wisdom. 14But if you are bitterly jealous and there is selfish ambition in your heart, don't cover up the truth with boasting and lying. 15For jealousy and selfishness are not God's kind of wisdom. Such things are earthly, unspiritual, and demonic. 16For wherever there is jealousy and selfish ambition, there you will find disorder and evil of every kind.

17But the wisdom from above is first of all pure. It is also peace loving, gentle at all times, and willing to yield to others. It is full of mercy and good deeds. It shows no favoritism and is always sincere. 18And those who are peacemakers will plant seeds of peace and reap a harvest of righteousness.*

3:6 Or *for it will burn in hell* (Greek *Gehenna*). **3:12** Greek *from salt.* **3:18** Or *of good things,* or *of justice.*

SPEECH	When our speech is motivated by	It is full of
	Satan	Bitter jealousy
		Selfish ambition
		Earthly concerns and desires
		Unspiritual thoughts and ideas
		Disorder
		Evil
	God and his wisdom	Purity
		Peace
		Consideration for others
		Submission
		Mercy
		Sincerity, impartiality
		Goodness

• **3:6** James compares the damage the tongue can do to a raging fire—the tongue's wickedness has its source in hell itself. The uncontrolled tongue can do terrible damage. Satan uses the tongue to divide people and pit them against one another. Idle and hateful words are damaging because they spread destruction quickly, and no one can stop the results once they are spoken. We dare not be careless with what we say, thinking we can apologize later, because even if we do, the scars remain. A few words spoken in anger can destroy a relationship that took years to build. Before you speak, remember that words are like fire—you can neither control nor reverse the damage they can do.

• **3:8** If no human being can tame the tongue, why bother trying? Even though we may not achieve perfect control of our tongues, the Holy Spirit will help us learn self-control. Remember that we are not fighting the tongue's fire in our own strength. The Holy Spirit will give us increasing power to monitor and control what we say, so that when we are offended, the Spirit will remind us of God's love, and we won't react in a hateful manner. When we are criticized, the Spirit will heal the hurt and help us to not lash out.

• **3:9-12** Our contradictory speech often puzzles us. At times our words are right and pleasing to God, but at other times they are violent and destructive. Which of these speech patterns reflects our true identity? We were made in God's image, but the tongue gives us a picture of our basic sinful nature. God works to change us from the inside out. When the Holy Spirit purifies a heart, he gives self-control so that the person will speak words that please God.

• **3:13-18** Have you ever known anyone who claimed to be wise but who acted foolishly? True wisdom can be measured by a person's character. Just as you can identify a tree by the type of fruit it produces, you can evaluate your wisdom by the way you act. Foolishness leads to disorder, but wisdom leads to peace and goodness. Are you tempted to escalate the conflict, pass on the gossip, or fan the fire of discord? Careful, winsome speech and wise, loving words are the seeds of peace. God loves peacemakers (Matthew 5:9).

• **3:14, 15** Bitter jealousy and selfish ambition are inspired by the devil. It is easy for us to be drawn into wrong desires by the pressures of society and sometimes even by well-meaning Christians. By listening to the advice: "Assert yourself," "Go for it," "Set high goals," we can be drawn into greed and destructive competitiveness. Seeking God's wisdom delivers us from the need to compare ourselves to others and to want what they have.

Drawing Close to God

4 What is causing the quarrels and fights among you? Don't they come from the evil desires at war within you? ²You want what you don't have, so you scheme and kill to get it. You are jealous of what others have, but you can't get it, so you fight and wage war to take it away from them. Yet you don't have what you want because you don't ask God for it. ³And even when you ask, you don't get it because your motives are all wrong—you want only what will give you pleasure.

⁴You adulterers!* Don't you realize that friendship with the world makes you an enemy of God? I say it again: If you want to be a friend of the world, you make yourself an enemy of God. ⁵What do you think the Scriptures mean when they say that the spirit God has placed within us is filled with envy?* ⁶But he gives us even more grace to stand against such evil desires. As the Scriptures say,

> "God opposes the proud
> but favors the humble."*

⁷So humble yourselves before God. Resist the devil, and he will flee from you. ⁸Come close to God, and God will come close to you. Wash your hands, you sinners; purify your hearts, for your loyalty is divided between God and the world. ⁹Let there be tears for what you have done. Let there be sorrow and deep grief. Let there be sadness instead of laughter, and gloom instead of joy. ¹⁰Humble yourselves before the Lord, and he will lift you up in honor.

Warning against Judging Others

¹¹Don't speak evil against each other, dear brothers and sisters.* If you criticize and judge each other, then you are criticizing and judging God's law. But your job is to obey the law, not to judge whether it applies to you. ¹²God alone, who gave the law, is the Judge. He alone has the power to save or to destroy. So what right do you have to judge your neighbor?

4:2
1 Jn 3:15
4:3
1 Jn 3:22; 5:14
4:4
John 15:19
1 Jn 2:15
4:5
1 Cor 6:19
2 Cor 6:16
4:6
†Prov 3:34
Matt 23:12
1 Pet 5:5
4:7
Eph 6:12
1 Pet 5:6-9
4:8
Ps 73:28
Isa 1:16
Zech 1:3
Mal 3:7
4:9
Luke 6:25
4:10
Job 5:11
1 Pet 5:6
4:11
Matt 7:1
2 Cor 12:20
1 Pet 2:1
4:12
Matt 10:28
Rom 2:1; 14:4
Jas 5:9

4:4 Greek *You adulteresses!*   **4:5** Or *that God longs jealously for the human spirit he has placed within us?* or *that the Holy Spirit, whom God has placed within us, opposes our envy?*   **4:6** Prov 3:34 (Greek version).   **4:11** Greek *brothers.*

• **4:1-3** Quarrels and fights among believers are always harmful. James explains that these conflicts result from evil desires battling within us: We want more possessions, more money, higher status, more recognition. When we don't get what we want, we fight in order to have it. Instead of aggressively grabbing what we want, we should submit ourselves to God, ask God to help us get rid of our selfish desires, and trust him to give us what we really need.

• **4:2, 3** James mentions the most common problems in prayer: not asking, asking for the wrong things, or asking for the wrong reasons. Do you talk to God at all? When you do, what do you talk about? Do you ask only to satisfy your desires? Do you seek God's approval for what you already plan to do? Your prayers will become powerful when you allow God to change your desires so that they perfectly correspond to his will for you (1 John 3:21, 22).

• **4:3, 4** There is nothing wrong with wanting a pleasurable life. God gives us good gifts that he wants us to enjoy (1:17; Ephesians 4:7; 1 Timothy 4:4, 5). But having friendship with the world involves seeking pleasure at others' expense or at the expense of obeying God. Pleasure that keeps us from pleasing God is sinful; pleasure from God's rich bounty is good.

• **4:4-6** The cure for evil desires is humility (see Proverbs 16:18, 19; 1 Peter 5:5, 6). Pride makes us self-centered and leads us to conclude that we deserve all we can see, touch, or imagine. It creates greedy appetites for far more than we need. We can be released from our self-centered desires by humbling ourselves before God, realizing that all we really need is his approval. When the Holy Spirit fills us, we see that this world's seductive attractions are only cheap substitutes for what God has to offer.

• **4:5** This verse may mean that because of our fallen nature, we have a tendency toward envy. James is not quoting a specific verse or passage—he is summing up a teaching of Scripture.

See Romans 6:6-8 and Galatians 5:17-21 for more on the human tendency toward envy and discontent.

• **4:7** Although God and the devil are at war, we don't have to wait until the end to see who will win. God has *already* defeated Satan (Revelation 12:10-12), and when Christ returns, the devil and all he stands for will be eliminated forever (Revelation 20:10-15). Satan is here now, however, and he is trying to win us over to his evil cause. With the Holy Spirit's power, we can resist the devil, and he will flee from us.

4:7-10 How can you come close to God? James gives five ways: (1) *Humble yourselves before God* (4:7). Yield to his authority and will, commit your life to him and his control, and be willing to follow him. (2) *Resist the devil* (4:7). Don't allow Satan to entice and tempt you. (3) *Wash your hands . . . and purify your hearts* (that is, lead a pure life) (4:8). Be cleansed from sin, replacing your desire to sin with your desire to experience God's purity. (4) *Let there be sorrow and deep grief* for your sins (4:9). Don't be afraid to express deep heartfelt sorrow for what you have done. (5) *Humble yourselves before the Lord,* and he will lift you up in honor (4:10; 1 Peter 5:6).

• **4:10** Bowing in humility before the Lord means recognizing that our worth comes from God alone. To be humble involves leaning on his power and his guidance, and not going our own independent way. Although we do not deserve God's favor, he wants to lift us up and give us worth and dignity, despite our human shortcomings.

4:11, 12 Jesus summarized the law as love for God and neighbor (Matthew 22:37-40), and Paul said that love demonstrated toward a neighbor would fully satisfy the law (Romans 13:6-10). When we fail to love, we are actually breaking God's law. Examine your attitude and actions toward others. Do you build people up or tear them down? When you're ready to criticize someone, remember God's law of love and say something good instead. Saying something beneficial to others will cure you of finding fault and increase your ability to obey God's law of love.

4:13-14
Prov 27:1
Luke 12:18-20

4:15
Acts 18:21

4:16
1 Cor 5:6

4:17
Luke 12:47

Warning about Self-Confidence

¹³Look here, you who say, "Today or tomorrow we are going to a certain town and will stay there a year. We will do business there and make a profit." ¹⁴How do you know what your life will be like tomorrow? Your life is like the morning fog—it's here a little while, then it's gone. ¹⁵What you ought to say is, "If the Lord wants us to, we will live and do this or that." ¹⁶Otherwise you are boasting about your own plans, and all such boasting is evil.

¹⁷Remember, it is sin to know what you ought to do and then not do it.

5:1
Prov 11:4, 28
Isa 13:6

5:2
Matt 6:19

Warning to the Rich

5 Look here, you rich people: Weep and groan with anguish because of all the terrible troubles ahead of you. ²Your wealth is rotting away, and your fine clothes are moth-eaten rags. ³Your gold and silver have become worthless. The very wealth you were counting

---

FAITH THAT WORKS
James offers a larger number of similarities to the Sermon on the Mount than any other book in the New Testament. James relied heavily on Jesus' teachings.

Lesson	Reference
When troubles come your way, consider it an opportunity for great joy.	James 1:2 Matthew 5:10-12
When your endurance is fully developed, you will be perfect and complete, needing nothing.	James 1:4 Matthew 5:48
Ask God, and he will answer.	James 1:5; 5:15 Matthew 7:7-12
Believers who are poor (who don't amount to much by the world's standards) should be glad, for God has honored them.	James 1:9 Matthew 5:3
Watch out for your anger. . . . It can be dangerous.	James 1:19, 20 Matthew 5:22
Be merciful to others, as God is merciful to you.	James 2:13 Matthew 5:7; 6:14
Your faith must express itself in your actions.	James 2:14-16 Matthew 7:21-23
Blessed are the peacemakers; they plant seeds of peace and reap a harvest of righteousness.	James 3:17, 18 Matthew 5:9
Friendship with the world makes you an enemy of God.	James 4:4 Matthew 6:24
When you humble yourself and realize your dependence on God, he will lift you up.	James 4:10 Matthew 5:3, 4
Don't speak evil against each other. If you do, you are criticizing and judging God's law.	James 4:11 Matthew 7:1, 2
Treasures on earth will only rot away and be eaten by moths. Store up eternal treasures in heaven.	James 5:2, 3 Matthew 6:19
Be patient in suffering, as God's prophets were patient.	James 5:10 Matthew 5:12
Be honest in your speech; just say a simple yes or no so that you will not sin.	James 5:12 Matthew 5:33-37

• **4:13-16** It is good to have goals, but goals can disappoint us if we leave God out of them. There is no point in making plans as though God does not exist because the future is in his hands. The beginning of good planning is to ask: "What would I like to be doing ten years from now? One year from now? Tomorrow? How will I react if God steps in and rearranges my plans?" We can plan ahead, but we must hold on to our plans loosely. If we put God's desires at the center of our planning, he will never disappoint us.

• **4:14** Life is short no matter how many years we live. Don't be deceived into thinking that you have lots of remaining time to live for Christ, to enjoy your loved ones, or to do what you know you should. Live for God today! Then, no matter when your life ends, you will have fulfilled God's plan for you.

• **4:17** We tend to think that *doing* wrong is sin. But James tells us that sin is also *not* doing right. (These two kinds of sin are sometimes called sins of commission and sins of omission.) It is a sin to lie; it can also be a sin to know the truth and not tell it. It is a sin to speak evil of someone; it is also a sin to avoid that person

when you know he or she needs your friendship. You should be willing to help as the Holy Spirit guides you. If God has directed you to do a kind act, to render a service, or to restore a relationship, do it. You will experience a renewed and refreshed vitality to your Christian faith.

• **5:1-6** James proclaims the worthlessness of riches, not the worthlessness of the rich. Today's money will be worthless when Christ returns, so we should spend our time accumulating the kind of treasures that will be worthwhile in God's eternal Kingdom. Money is not the problem; Christian leaders need money to live and to support their families; missionaries need money to help them spread the Good News; churches need money to do their work effectively. It is the *love* of money that leads to evil (1 Timothy 6:10) and causes some people to oppress others in order to get more. This is a warning to all Christians who are tempted to adopt worldly standards rather than God's standards (Romans 12:1, 2) as well as an encouragement to all those who are oppressed by the rich. Also read Matthew 6:19-21 to see what Jesus says about riches.

on will eat away your flesh like fire. This treasure you have accumulated will stand as evidence against you on the day of judgment. ⁴For listen! Hear the cries of the field workers whom you have cheated of their pay. The wages you held back cry out against you. The cries of those who harvest your fields have reached the ears of the LORD of Heaven's Armies.

⁵You have spent your years on earth in luxury, satisfying your every desire. You have fattened yourselves for the day of slaughter. ⁶You have condemned and killed innocent people,* who do not resist you.*

Patience and Endurance

⁷Dear brothers and sisters,* be patient as you wait for the Lord's return. Consider the farmers who patiently wait for the rains in the fall and in the spring. They eagerly look for the valuable harvest to ripen. ⁸You, too, must be patient. Take courage, for the coming of the Lord is near.

⁹Don't grumble about each other, brothers and sisters, or you will be judged. For look— the Judge is standing at the door!

¹⁰For examples of patience in suffering, dear brothers and sisters, look at the prophets who spoke in the name of the Lord. ¹¹We give great honor to those who endure under suffering. For instance, you know about Job, a man of great endurance. You can see how the Lord was kind to him at the end, for the Lord is full of tenderness and mercy.

¹²But most of all, my brothers and sisters, never take an oath, by heaven or earth or anything else. Just say a simple yes or no, so that you will not sin and be condemned.

The Power of Prayer

¹³Are any of you suffering hardships? You should pray. Are any of you happy? You should sing praises. ¹⁴Are any of you sick? You should call for the elders of the church to come and pray over you, anointing you with oil in the name of the Lord. ¹⁵Such a prayer offered in faith will heal the sick, and the Lord will make you well. And if you have committed any sins, you will be forgiven.

¹⁶Confess your sins to each other and pray for each other so that you may be healed. The

5:4
Lev 19:13
Deut 24:14-15
Ps 18:6
Isa 5:9

5:5
Jer 12:3; 25:34
Luke 16:19-23

5:7
Deut 11:14
Jer 5:24
Joel 2:23

5:8
Rom 13:11-12
Heb 10:37

5:9
Matt 24:33
1 Cor 4:5
Jas 4:12

5:11
Job 1:20-22;
2:7-10; 42:10-17
Ps 103:8

5:12
Matt 5:34-37

5:13
Col 3:16

5:14
Mark 6:13

5:15
Mark 16:18
Jas 1:6

5:16
Matt 18:15-18
1 Jn 1:9

5:6a Or *killed the Righteous One.* **5:6b** Or *Don't they resist you?* or *Doesn't God oppose you?* or *Aren't they now accusing you before God?* **5:7** Greek *brothers;* also in 5:9, 10, 12, 19.

• **5:6** "Innocent people" refers to defenseless persons, probably poor laborers. Poor people who could not pay their debts were thrown in prison or forced to sell all their possessions. At times, they were even forced to sell their family members into slavery. With no opportunity to work off their debts, poor people often died of starvation. God called this murder. Hoarding money, exploiting employees, and living self-indulgently will not escape God's notice.

• **5:7, 8** The farmer must wait patiently for his crops to grow; he cannot hurry the process. But he does not take the summer off and hope that all goes well in the fields. There is much work to do to ensure a good harvest. In the same way, we must wait patiently for Christ's return. We cannot make him come back any sooner. But while we wait, there is much work that we can do to advance God's Kingdom. Both the farmer and the Christian must live by faith, looking toward the future reward for their labors. Don't live as if Christ will never come. Work faithfully to build his Kingdom. The King *will* come when the time is right.

• **5:9** When things go wrong, we tend to grumble against and blame others for our miseries (see the second note on Genesis 3:11-13). Blaming others is easier than owning our share of the responsibility, but it can be both destructive and sinful. Before you judge others for their shortcomings, remember that Christ the Judge will come to evaluate each of us (Matthew 7:1-5; 25:31-46). He will not let us get away with shifting the blame to others.

5:10, 11 Many prophets suffered and were persecuted, such as Moses, Elijah, and Jeremiah. For a complete list of those persecuted, see the chart in 2 Chronicles 18, pp. 690-691. For more on the topic of suffering, see the notes on Job 1:1ff; 2:10; 3:23-26; 4:7, 8; 42:17; and Job's Profile in Job 3, p. 789.

5:12 A person with a reputation for exaggeration or lying often can't get anyone to believe him on his word alone. Christians should never become like that. Always be honest so that others will believe your simple yes or no. By avoiding lies, half-truths, and omissions of the truth, you will become known as a trustworthy person.

• **5:14, 15** James is referring to someone who is physically ill. In Scripture, oil was both a medicine (see the parable of the Good Samaritan in Luke 10:30-37) and a symbol of the Spirit of God (as used in anointing kings, see 1 Samuel 16:1-13). Thus, oil can represent both the medical and the spiritual spheres of life. Christians should not separate the physical and the spiritual. Jesus Christ is Lord over both the body and the spirit.

• **5:14, 15** People in the church are not alone. Members of Christ's body should be able to count on others for support and prayer, especially when they are sick or suffering. The elders should be on call to respond to the illness of any member, and the church should be sensitive to the needs of all its members.

• **5:15** The "prayer offered in faith" does not refer to the faith of the sick person but to the faith of the people praying. God heals, faith doesn't, and all prayers are subject to God's will. But prayer is part of God's healing process.

• **5:16** Christ has made it possible for us to go directly to God for forgiveness. But confessing our sins to each other still has an important place in the life of the church. (1) If we have sinned against an individual, we must ask him or her to forgive us. (2) If our sin has affected the church, we must confess it publicly. (3) If we need loving support as we struggle with a sin, we should confess that sin to those who are able to provide that support. (4) If we doubt God's forgiveness, after confessing a sin to him, we may wish to confess that sin to a fellow believer for assurance of God's pardon. In Christ's Kingdom, every believer is a priest to other believers (1 Peter 2:9).

5:17
1 Kgs 17:1-7
Luke 4:25

5:18
1 Kgs 18:42-45

earnest prayer of a righteous person has great power and produces wonderful results. [17]Elijah was as human as we are, and yet when he prayed earnestly that no rain would fall, none fell for three and a half years! [18]Then, when he prayed again, the sky sent down rain and the earth began to yield its crops.

5:19
Matt 18:15

5:20
Prov 10:12
1 Pet 4:8

Restore Wandering Believers

[19]My dear brothers and sisters, if someone among you wanders away from the truth and is brought back, [20]you can be sure that whoever brings the sinner back will save that person from death and bring about the forgiveness of many sins.

• **5:16-18** The Christian's most powerful resource is communion with God through prayer. The results are often greater than we thought were possible. Some people see prayer as a last resort to be tried when all else fails. This approach is backward. Prayer should come first. Because God's power is infinitely greater than ours, it only makes sense to rely on it—especially because God encourages us to do so.

5:17 For more about the great prophet Elijah, read his Profile in 1 Kings 17, p. 545.

• **5:19, 20** Clearly this person who has wandered from the truth is a believer who has fallen into sin—one who is no longer living a life consistent with his or her beliefs. Christians disagree over whether or not it is possible for people to lose their salvation, but all agree that those who fall away from their faith are in serious

trouble and need to repent. James urges Christians to help back-sliders return to God. By taking the initiative, praying for the person, and acting in love, we can meet the person where he or she is and bring him or her back to God and his forgiveness.

• **5:20** The book of James emphasizes faith in action. Right living is the evidence and result of faith. The church must serve with compassion, speak lovingly and truthfully, live in obedience to God's commands, and love one another. The body of believers ought to be an example of heaven on earth, drawing people to Christ through love for God and each other. If we truly believe God's Word, we will *live* it day by day. God's Word is not merely something we read or think about, but something we do. Belief, faith, and trust must have hands and feet—ours!

STUDY QUESTIONS

Thirteen lessons for individual or group study

It's always exciting to get more than you expect. And that's what you'll find in this Bible study guide—much more than you expect. Our goal was to write thoughtful, practical, dependable, and application-oriented studies of God's word.

This study guide contains the complete text of the selected Bible book. The commentary is accurate, complete, and loaded with unique charts and other Bible helps.

With the Bible text, extensive notes and helps, and questions to guide discussion, *Life Application Bible Studies* have everything you need in one place.

The lessons in this Bible study guide will work for large classes as well as small-group studies. To get everyone involved in your discussions, encourage participants to answer the questions before each meeting.

Each lesson is divided into five easy-to-lead sections. The section called "Reflect" introduces you and the members of your group to a specific area of life touched by the lesson. "Read" shows which chapters to read and which notes and other features to use. Additional questions help you understand the passage. "Realize" brings into focus the biblical principle to be learned with questions, a special insight, or both. "Respond" helps you make connections with your own situation and personal needs. The questions are designed to help you find areas in your life where you can apply the biblical truths. "Resolve" helps you map out action plans for that day.

Begin and end each lesson with prayer, asking for the Holy Spirit's guidance, direction, and wisdom.

Recommended time allotments for each section of a lesson are as follows:

Segment	60 minutes	90 minutes
Reflect on your life	*5 minutes*	*10 minutes*
Read the passage	*10 minutes*	*15 minutes*
Realize the principle	*15 minutes*	*20 minutes*
Respond to the message	*20 minutes*	*30 minutes*
Resolve to take action	*10 minutes*	*15 minutes*

All five sections work together to help a person learn the lessons, live out the principles, and obey the commands taught in the Bible.

Also, at the end of each lesson, there is a section entitled "More for studying other themes in this section." These questions will help you lead the group in studying other parts of each section not covered in depth by the main lesson.

But don't just listen to God's word. You must do what it says. Otherwise you are only fooling yourselves. For if you listen to the word and don't obey, it is like glancing at your face in a mirror. You see yourself, walk away, and forget what you look like. But if you look carefully into the perfect law that sets you free, and if you do what it says and don't forget what you heard, then God will bless you for doing it (James 1:22-25).

LESSON 1
TALK IS CHEAP
JAMES INTRODUCTION

REFLECT
on your life

1 When shopping, when do you prefer a clone, or generic substitute, over a name brand? On what items do you prefer to stick with the name brand?

_____

_____

_____

2 What is the difference between an original work of art and a print? In general, why do people prefer the genuine article?

_____

_____

_____

READ
the passage

Read the introduction to James, the chart "Faith That Works" on page 11, James 1:1, and the following notes:

❐ 1:1   ❐ 5:20

3 What do you know about the author of this letter?

_____

_____

_____

4 What audience was James addressing? What do you know about their situation?

_____

_____

_____

5 How does this setting compare to your situation?

_____

_____

_____

6 On the chart, which of the similarities to the Sermon on the Mount surprises you the most?

_____

_____

_____

7 List five of the topics covered in James, in order of interest to you.

a. _____

b. _____

c. _____

d. _____

e. _____

8 Why will genuine Christian faith always show itself in the life of a person?

_____

_____

REALIZE
the principle

The letter of James is a powerful argument for putting faith into practice. It dramatically demonstrates the relevancy of the Christian faith to all of life. Whether Christians are at home, with neighbors, at work, or at church, there should be a consistency evident in their faith. As important as it is to know true theology and the content of God's word, knowledge alone is insufficient. Even talking about it is not enough. We must also apply what we know to everyday life. Genuine faith always shows through in the life of a believer. Be prepared for a challenging and stimulating adventure as you study the letter of James and discover the implications that faith has for your life.

9 How can a person know that his or her faith is the genuine article, the real thing?

_____

_____

_____

10 James was concerned because many Christians of his day were satisfied that intellectual agreement with Christianity was enough. To what extent is this a problem today?

_____

_____

_____

11 What is the problem with mere intellectual agreement?

_____

_____

_____

12 What are some of the cheap substitutes for genuine faith?

_____

_____

_____

13 What are some of the dangers of emphasizing a changed life as proof of genuine faith?

_____

_____

_____

14 What can the church do to help Christians put their faith into practice?

_____

_____

_____

_____

15 What would happen if you were in a country where you could not speak openly about your faith—how might others know you were a Christian?

_____

_____

_____

_____

16 In what areas of your life do you find it easy to talk about but difficult to live out your faith?

RESOLVE
to take action

_____

_____

_____

_____

17 Be honest and take a good look at the actions that flow from your life. Apart from your words, what evidences of faith are there in your life? If actions speak louder than words, what are your actions saying?

_____

_____

_____

_____

A Study the "Faith That Works" chart. What is the relationship between the book of James and the Sermon on the Mount? What do you think accounts for James's offering a larger number of similarities than any other book in the New Testament?

MORE
for studying
other themes
in this section

B James describes genuine faith. What was the imitation faith of that day? What imitations do we see in and around the church today?

C How do you know that you are a child of God? What role do good deeds play in giving you assurance?

D Compare James to Proverbs and Ecclesiastes. Why are these three books called wisdom literature? What are the relative strengths of each?

LESSON 2
WHEN THE GOING GETS TOUGH . . .
JAMES 1: 2-12

R

REFLECT
on your life

1 Describe a moment of pure joy in your life. What did you do? What happened? How did you react?

_____

_____

_____

_____

_____

2 When have you had to persevere to reach a goal? What kept you going? How did this experience change you for the better?

_____

_____

_____

_____

R

READ
the passage

Read James 1:2-12 and the following notes:

❏ 1:2, 3   ❏ 1:2-4   ❏ 1:5   ❏ 1:6   ❏ 1:6-8   ❏ 1:12

3 How can trials be helpful to us (1:3-4)?

_____

_____

_____

_____

4 What kind of help does God provide for Christians when they endure trials (1:5)?

_____

_____

_____

5 How is a trial different from a temptation?

_____

_____

_____

6 If trials can be so beneficial, why don't we look forward to them?

_____

_____

_____

7 Why is it difficult to respond to trials with joy?

_____

_____

_____

REALIZE
the principle

James teaches that God's purpose is to develop Christians who are mature and complete. If it were up to us, that process probably wouldn't include times of stress, hardship, or testing. But God knows us well, and as our loving Father he knows that our faith and character are developed only through trials and testing. The apostle Paul's teaching in Romans 8:28 makes such a practical difference when we face difficult trials. "And we know that God causes everything to work together for the good of those who love God and are called according to his purpose for them." Although we might be tempted to turn away from God and run from him during our trials, knowing God's love and remembering his purpose in them can help us to trust him even more.

8 List some typical kinds of trials in the life of a Christian. Be careful to distinguish between a trial and a temptation.

_____

_____

_____

_____

RESPOND
to the message

9 Describe the difference between having a short-term and a long-term perspective on trials.

_____

_____

_____

_____

10 Think of someone who has had a difficult life. What has helped that person persevere? What did that person learn through it? What did that person's experience teach you?

_____

_____

_____

_____

11 When did you experience the most difficult period of your life? What kept you going through it? What did you learn through it?

_____

_____

_____

_____

_____

12 What trials are you currently facing?

_____

_____

_____

_____

13 What would help you respond to your trials with real joy?

_____

_____

_____

_____

14 Responding to trials can be difficult when you are alone. Who could meet with you regularly to help you and pray for you during a difficult time in your life?

RESOLVE
to take action

_____

_____

_____

_____

15 Think of a specific trial you are facing right now. Write down several possibilities for how God may be using it in your life. Ask God for the ability to respond to the trial with trust in him and in his plan for you.

_____

_____

_____

_____

_____

A What does it mean to ask without doubting (1:6-8)? How is this different from humility and uncertainty?

MORE
for studying
other themes
in this section

B What does 1:9-11 have to do with the theme of enduring trials? How could having an eternal perspective on trials help you bear your struggles?

C James wrote that the crown of life is given to those who persevere (1:12). How does perseverance relate to salvation through faith? What is the relationship between faith and deeds?

D James says that the promise of a crown of life is an incentive to respond to trials in a positive way. How does this promise of future blessing really make any difference for us?

E Abraham faced a great test of his faith when he was asked to sacrifice his only son. Why does God test the faith of his people? How has your faith been tested?

LESSON 3
EXCUSES, EXCUSES
JAMES 1:13-18

REFLECT
on your life

1 What is one of the funniest excuses that you have ever heard a small child try to use?

_____

_____

2 Describe a time in your childhood when you tried to blame someone else for a problem that you really caused. Did you get away with it? What happened?

_____

_____

_____

READ
the passage

Read James 1:13-18 and the following notes:

❏ 1:12-15   ❏ 1:13, 14   ❏ 1:13-15

3 What two arguments does James use here to demonstrate that God is not the source of temptation?

_____

_____

_____

4 What is the ultimate source of temptation?

_____

_____

5 Why is temptation so dangerous?

_____

_____

_____

6 How is it possible for Christians to be deceived?

_____

_____

_____

7 How are temptations different from trials?

_____

_____

_____

REALIZE
the principle

Temptations come from our own sinful desires as we are attracted and inflamed by the world's values, people, and pleasures. These temptations lead us into sin and away from God. It should not be surprising, then, that we often try to blame God as the source of our temptations. This kind of attitude drives us even further away from God. Don't be deceived—shifting the blame will cause you to doubt God's goodness.

8 God does not tempt us, but he will test our faith. Explain this statement.

_____

_____

_____

_____

9 If God really does love his people, why doesn't he protect them from temptations?

_____

_____

_____

RESPOND
to the message

10 When temptation comes, why do people tend to blame others and excuse themselves instead of taking responsibility for their sin and their actions?

_____

_____

_____

_____

11 What might cause people to blame God for their temptations?

_____

_____

_____

12 Other than blaming God when we are tempted, what are some other ways we avoid taking responsibility for our own actions?

_____

_____

_____

13 What specific activities awaken and encourage your sinful desires and lead to temptation? (For example, for some people it may be browsing at a magazine rack, watching certain television shows or movies, or envying others.)

_____

_____

_____

14 In what ways do you avoid taking responsibility for your sin? What favorite excuses do you find yourself using?

_____

_____

_____

15 What can you do to prevent yourself from falling into temptation?

_____

_____

_____

16 What are some appropriate ways for Christians to respond after they have given in to temptation?

_____

_____

17 What resources has God given you for resisting and defeating temptation?

RESOLVE
to take action

_____

_____

_____

_____

18 Think of one particular area of your life where you are consistently being tempted and led into sin. How can you stop excusing yourself? What can you do to prevent this from happening?

_____

_____

_____

_____

A What is Satan's role in the process of temptation? How can you resist his efforts in your life?

MORE
for studying
other themes
in this section

B What are some examples of being tempted but not sinning? How can you know when you are crossing the line?

C What ways does Satan use to lead churches into temptation and sin? What are some specific areas of concern for your local church?

D Why do you think James emphasized the goodness of God (1:17)? What good gifts has God given you that help you feel his love?

E What did James mean when he called his readers God's "prized possession" (1:18)? Why do you think he used this phrase to describe believers?

LESSON 4
JUST DO IT!
JAMES 1:19-27

REFLECT
on your life

1 When have you given someone advice only to have that person completely ignore it to his or her own peril? Why didn't that person do what you suggested?

_____

_____

_____

_____

2 Think of a time recently when you looked as though you were listening to someone but the words were going in one ear and out the other. What were you thinking about instead?

_____

_____

_____

_____

READ
the passage

Read James 1:19-27 and the following notes:

❐ 1:19   ❐ 1:19, 20   ❐ 1:22-25   ❐ 1:25   ❐ 1:27

3 How do believers deceive themselves by just listening to God's word (1:22)?

_____

_____

_____

_____

4 What do you use a mirror for throughout the day? How is the Bible like a mirror for us (1:23-25)?

_____

_____

_____

_____

5 How can God's law bring freedom (1:25)?

_____

_____

_____

_____

6 Most believers will say that the Bible is the most important book in their life. Why, then, is it so easy for us to almost immediately forget what we hear or read in the Bible?

REALIZE
the principle

_____

_____

_____

_____

As important as it is to read the Bible, James teaches us that it is not helpful unless we do what it says. It's been said that it's not enough to "talk the talk"; we must "walk the walk." That's the concern James has for us. As important as it is to know God's word and to be eager learners in personal Bible study and in church, it is equally important to be living out what we believe. Genuine faith will evidence itself in some very practical ways: in righteous living, godly speaking, and compassionate care. Does your lifestyle reflect your Christian faith? Whether you are at church, at a neighborhood gathering, or in the marketplace, people should see a consistency between what you say and how you live. Revelation demands response! Don't fall into the trap of reading or listening to the Bible and then not putting it into practice.

7 What might be the effects in the life of a person who reads the Bible week after week but never puts any of the truths into practice?

_____

_____

_____

_____

RESPOND
to the message

8 In what ways does your church need to be more consistent in putting into practice what it teaches and believes?

_____

_____

_____

_____

9 Why is it often difficult to pay attention to the reading of Scripture in church? What would help you to pay closer attention?

_____

_____

_____

_____

10 What keeps you from doing what you read in the Bible? How could you make a closer link between what you read and how you behave?

_____

_____

_____

_____

_____

11 What steps do you take to apply the Bible to your life?

_____

_____

_____

_____

12 What can you do to put the truths of the Bible into practice?

RESOLVE
to take action

_____

_____

_____

A How is it possible to keep a tight rein on the tongue? What resources does God provide that might be helpful for you?

MORE
for studying
other themes
in this section

B Which of the following is most difficult for you: listening intently to people, being slow to speak, or being slow to get angry?

C How is a concern for getting rid of all the "filth and evil" related to political and social action? What are some current issues in your local community on which a Christian might take a stand?

D How is "refusing to let the world corrupt you" possible? What preventative steps are you taking now?

E What is so significant about having a desire to care for orphans and widows (1:27)? Why would James highlight it as a mark of genuine faith?

F What groups of people might be included in the admonition to care for orphans and widows? What are some practical ways that you, and your church, can care for the orphans and widows of your world? Who are the orphans and widows in your life?

LESSON 5
PLAYING FAVORITES
JAMES 2:1-13

REFLECT
on your life

1 Describe a situation in which a teacher showed favoritism in class. How did the class know about it? How did you feel about it?

_____

_____

_____

_____

2 In what ways do adults continue to play favorites at home, at work, or in government?

_____

_____

_____

READ
the passage

Read James 2:1-13 and the following notes:

❏ 2:1ff   ❏ 2:1-7   ❏ 2:2-4   ❏ 2:5   ❏ 2:8, 9   ❏ 2:12   ❏ 2:13

3 Why is favoritism to the rich inconsistent with believing in Christ (2:1-4)?

_____

_____

_____

4 What is God's attitude toward the poor (2:5)?

_____

_____

5 How does loving your neighbor as yourself relate to showing favoritism at church (2:8-9)?

_____

_____

_____

6 Why are the rich usually treated with special favor in the world?

_____

_____

_____

REALIZE
the principle

James is echoing the consistent teaching of the Old and New Testaments in this passage—that God has a heart of compassion for the poor and destitute. He is rich in mercy, a God who delights in caring for those who don't count for much in the world's eyes. All Christians have received undeserved mercy from God and are called by God to express mercy to those in need. That's why favoritism to the rich is so unacceptable: It values that which God says is unimportant. Be very careful in your personal life and in your church to treat people according to God's values rather than by the values of the world.

7 Today most churches would not usher people to good or bad seats. But in what other ways might people favor the rich at church?

_____

_____

_____

8 For what reasons do people show favoritism to the poor?

_____

_____

_____

RESPOND
to the message

9 In what ways does God show favoritism to the poor?

_____

_____

_____

_____

10 How does God's view of wealth compare with your view? In what specific areas do you need to align your thinking about wealth and poverty with God's?

_____

_____

_____

_____

_____

11 Would a poor person feel accepted in your church? Why?

_____

_____

_____

_____

12 In what ways do you favor some people over others at church?

_____

_____

_____

_____

13 Whom have you snubbed or favored, perhaps without being aware of it at the time? Why did you do it?

_____

_____

_____

_____

_____

14 In what other ways can you apply this principle of not showing favoritism on the basis of what the world considers important?

_____

_____

_____

_____

_____

15 Think of someone whom God has brought into your life who is unattractive or seems to have little to offer you. Perhaps you have been guilty of ignoring this person in the past. Ask God to help you see this person more clearly from his perspective. List at least three specific actions you can take to reach out to this person with Christ's love.

RESOLVE
to take action

_____

_____

_____

_____

_____

_____

A Are riches ever a sign of God's favor? How much of your prayer life is given to pursuing material requests?

MORE
for studying
other themes
in this section

B Why do you think God gives such priority to the poor? Why doesn't God simply bless them with more material things? Why doesn't God always answer your prayers for material blessings?

C Who will receive mercy from God (2:5)? How does this relate to salvation by faith alone? In what areas of your life has your faith led you to be more merciful?

D Why does James call the command to "love your neighbor as yourself" the "royal law" (2:8)? In what ways does it summarize all the laws governing human relationships? What changes would this make in how you interact with your spouse, children, or a close friend?

E Why is a person who breaks just one of God's laws guilty of breaking all of them (2:10-11)?

LESSON 6
NOW GET TO WORK!
JAMES 2:14-26

REFLECT
on your life

1 How do you feel about salespeople who try to sell you something that they probably wouldn't use themselves? What do you think of people who don't believe in their product?

_____

_____

_____

_____

2 When have you had to do something that you didn't believe in? What kept you going?

_____

_____

_____

_____

READ
the passage

Read James 2:14-26 and the following notes:

❐ 2:14   ❐ 2:17   ❐ 2:18   ❐ 2:21-24   ❐ 2:25

3 What does James teach about the relationship between faith and deeds? What argument might James be countering?

_____

_____

_____

_____

4 Why can't we separate faith from deeds (2:18-19)? How do people try to separate them today?

_____

_____

_____

5 In what ways are Abraham and Rahab different? In what ways are they similar (2:21-25)?

_____

_____

_____

_____

6 If we are saved by faith alone, why are deeds important?

_____

_____

_____

REALIZE
the principle

The relationship between faith and deeds is a very important theological topic. This was a major area of contention during the Reformation. The Bible clearly teaches that we are saved by faith in Christ alone (Romans 3:28; Galatians 2:15-16; Ephesians 2:8-9). When James says that a person is not justified by faith alone (2:24), he isn't contradicting Paul's teaching in Romans 3:28 ("So we are made right with God through faith and not by obeying the law"). James passionately challenges, stirs up, and admonishes all those who believe in Christ to put their faith into practice. Anything less would not be worthy of the God we serve and would not be genuine faith. When we become God's children by faith, God gives us a new heart (Ezekiel 36:25-26), and we become joined to Christ (John 15:5). Because of this, genuine faith in Christ will always produce thoughts, words, and deeds that reflect God's character and his lordship. The relationship between faith and lifestyle is inseparable. It isn't that we are saved on the basis of what we do. Rather, our deeds are the inevitable result and evidence of God's redeeming work in us.

7 What is the difference between a faith that is weak and a faith that is dead?

_____

_____

_____

_____

_____

R
RESPOND
to the message

8 What kind of reputation for faith in action does your church have in your community? If it's not what you would prefer, what might it take to improve that reputation?

_____

_____

_____

9 How would you answer a person who pointed to the life of Abraham as proof that we are saved by what we do?

_____

_____

_____

10 What would you say to a person who claimed to have faith in Christ but was living an unrepentant, ongoing lifestyle of sin?

_____

_____

_____

11 If you were on trial for being a Christian, what areas of your life would provide strong evidence of genuine faith?

_____

_____

_____

12 If you were on trial for being a Christian, what areas would provide insufficient evidence of genuine faith?

_____

_____

_____

13 What might be some consequences for believers who are not clear on the relationship between faith and works?

_____

_____

_____

_____

14 Each evening this week, remind yourself that you are saved by faith, not by what you do. Consider how you lived out your faith during that day. (How did your faith make a difference in what you did?) Then ask God to strengthen your faith.

RESOLVE
to take action

_____

_____

_____

_____

_____

_____

A What do you think demons know about God (2:19)? How can they have knowledge about God and still not follow him? What prevents you from following Christ when you have true knowledge?

MORE
for studying
other themes
in this section

B Some people think that Romans 3:28 and James 2:24 contradict each other. Is it possible for the Bible to contradict itself? What do you do when it seems that there is a contradiction?

C Why do you think Abraham was called God's friend? What did Jesus mean when he called those who follow him "my friends" (John 15:14)?

LESSON 7
UNBRIDLED POWER
JAMES 3:1-12

REFLECT
on your life

1 What is the most helpful, positive, or encouraging thing someone has said to you recently?

_____

_____

_____

2 Words have great power. Give some examples of the damaging power of words.

_____

_____

_____

READ
the passage

Read James 3:1-12 and the following notes:

❏ 3:2, 3   ❏ 3:6   ❏ 3:8   ❏ 3:9-12

3 Why is it so difficult for us to be careful in all that we say (3:2)?

_____

_____

4 James compares the tongue to a bit, a rudder, and a spark. What do all of these images have in common (3:3-6)?

_____

_____

5 What warnings does James give about the tongue? What positive results does he mention?

_____

_____

_____

6 If no person can tame the tongue, what hope is there for controlling it?

_____

_____

_____

REALIZE
the principle

Will we ever be able to control what we say? James says that the tongue corrupts the whole person, sets the whole course of life on fire, is a restless evil, and cannot be tamed. Yet we should not give up trying. James indicates in 3:2-6 that Christians should work on controlling their tongue. The difficulty with the tongue is that it is connected to the heart! As Jesus said in Matthew 12:34, "For whatever is in your heart determines what you say." A tongue problem is really a heart problem. But God specializes in heart problems, giving each Christian a new heart—one that is alive to God and sensitive to his leading. Then, as we turn from sin and learn to turn to God in faith and trust, God changes us on the inside, making us like Christ. Apart from God, no person can control the tongue, but with a new heart we can find a new strength to use our tongue to glorify God and to build up people around us.

7 How can someone praise God but still curse people?

_____

_____

8 What kind of damage can an uncontrolled tongue do to a family? to a marriage? to children? to a church?

_____

_____

RESPOND
to the message

9 What would you say to someone who professed faith in Christ but was either unwilling or seemingly unable to control his or her tongue?

_____

_____

_____

10 What kind of rationalizations have you used for having said hurtful words?

_____

_____

11 Who is the best example you know of someone who has control over what he or she says? How did that person acquire that kind of self-control?

_____

_____

_____

12 List some specific problems that Christians can have with what they say. Which of these do you consider the most offensive? Why?

_____

_____

13 Under what circumstances do you tend to speak in ways that contradict your praise on Sunday?

_____

_____

_____

14 In what practical ways do believers bring their speech under God's control?

_____

_____

_____

15 What kinds of support can a person find for help in this area?

_____

_____

_____

16 In what ways can we use our tongues positively?

_____

_____

_____

17 Of all the problems with the tongue mentioned above, choose the one that is the most obvious problem for you. With God's help, what small battles do you think you could win in this area this week?

RESOLVE
to take action

_____

_____

_____

_____

18 List the steps you will need to take, with God's help, to see some immediate improvement.

_____

_____

_____

_____

A In what way will teachers be judged more strictly (3:1)? How can you help those who teach you God's word?

MORE
for studying
other themes
in this section

B Why isn't the tongue problem solved when people become Christians? In what ways do you struggle with the tension between the old nature and the new nature?

C Is it possible for people to control themselves in every way (3:2)? Why do you think James made this statement?

D How should knowing that people are made in the image of God influence how you speak to them?

LESSON 8
WHAT DO YOU KNOW?
JAMES 3:13-18

REFLECT
on your life

1 List some of the most ambitious people you know. What are they like? What are their goals?

_____

_____

_____

_____

_____

2 List some of the wisest people you know. What evidence of wisdom have you seen in their life? What are their goals?

_____

_____

_____

_____

READ
the passage

Read James 3:13-18 and the following notes:

❒ 3:13-18   ❒ 3:14, 15

3 What are the characteristics of earthly wisdom?

_____

_____

_____

_____

4 How can you tell earthly wisdom from heavenly wisdom?

_____

_____

_____

_____

5 Why is earthly wisdom often mistaken for heavenly wisdom (3:17)?

_____

_____

_____

_____

_____

6 Why are jealousy and selfishness singled out as characteristics of earthly wisdom (3:15)?

REALIZE
the principle

_____

_____

_____

_____

The world praises those with ambition, and sometimes we admire them too. Most people think it's smart to be ambitious. Yet James draws a clear contrast between this kind of earthly wisdom and God's wisdom. They have dramatically different characteristics, orientations, and results. The world does a great job of packaging and marketing its own wisdom proudly, insistently, and without apology. That's the reason for Paul's warning in Romans 12:2: "Don't copy the behavior and customs of this world, but let God transform you into a new person by changing the way you think." Watch out for the seductiveness of the world's wisdom. Following it may seem like the smart thing to do, but that's not a wise choice.

7 How might a church make a decision based on earthly wisdom rather than God's wisdom?

_____

_____

_____

_____

8 List some examples of how earthly wisdom is packaged and presented on current television shows or ads.

_____

_____

_____

_____

_____

9 How might non-Christians defend earthly wisdom? What negative comments might they possibly have for the wisdom that comes from heaven?

_____

_____

_____

_____

_____

10 Why is selfish ambition a part of earthly wisdom? Is it ever right for a Christian to be ambitious?

_____

_____

_____

_____

_____

11 In what areas of your life are you most vulnerable to the world's wisdom?

_____

_____

_____

_____

12 Who can help you say no to the world's wisdom and yes to God's wisdom?

_____

_____

_____

_____

13 What practical steps can you take to gain more of God's wisdom?

RESOLVE
to take action

_____

_____

_____

_____

_____

14 Write out a prayer asking God to make you wise with the wisdom that comes from heaven. Pray this prayer each day this week.

_____

_____

_____

_____

_____

_____

A What is the significance of James putting the words _bitterly_ and _jealous_ together? How have you seen them come together in your life or in your church?

MORE
for studying
other themes
in this section

B What would prompt someone who was harboring selfish ambition and bitter jealousy to boast about it?

C What evil practices might result from earthly wisdom? What mechanism does your church have for dealing with such things?

D In describing the quality of God's wisdom, why does James say that it is "first of all pure"? What makes it difficult for us to have a wisdom that is pure?

E What does it mean to be a peacemaker (3:18)? How do peacemakers plant and reap?

LESSON 9
FIGHTS, QUARRELS, AND
OTHER CHURCH PASTIMES
JAMES 4:1-12

REFLECT
on your life

1 Circle any of the following that describe the way people fight at your church:

hand-to-hand combat   hijacking and other terrorist activities

bayonets and rifles   intelligence and espionage

tanks, planes, and missiles   negotiated peace with occasional skirmishes

guerrilla warfare   cold war

sniper attacks   "Who, me? I didn't do anything!"

booby traps and land mines   other: _____

2 What is your idea of a good, clean church fight?

_____

_____

_____

_____

READ
the passage

Read James 4:1-12 and the following notes:

❏ 4:1-3   ❏ 4:2, 3   ❏ 4:3, 4   ❏ 4:4-6   ❏ 4:5   ❏ 4:7   ❏ 4:10

3 What are some reasons that Christians don't get along with each other (4:1-2)?

_____

_____

_____

_____

4 What are the wrong motives for prayer (4:3)? With what motives should we pray?

_____

_____

_____

5 What does "friendship with the world" mean (4:4)?

_____

_____

6 How does James instruct us to deal with these problems (4:5-10)?

_____

_____

_____

7 Why do people fight over issues at church?

_____

_____   REALIZE
                                                                   the principle
_____

_____

James doesn't paint a pretty picture of life in the church. It sounds much like life anytime people are together: quarreling, fighting, slandering, judging. The difference is that there's hope for real change in the church. These problems arise when Christians exchange friendship with God for that of the world. As with all of Satan's treacheries, the world's friendship might sound good at first, but it will soon bring a harvest of sin, jealousy, hatred, and self-centeredness. The good news is that Christians have an alternative—to return to God in confession and dependency. God never tires of welcoming home his wayward children and of lifting them up when they humble themselves before him. If you find yourself constantly embroiled in disagreements and arguments, take a close look at your heart . . . and come home to friendship with God.

8 What is the connection between our relationship with God and our relationship with people?

_____

_____

_____

9 Why is it impossible to be a friend of the world and a friend of God at the same time?

_____

_____

_____

_____

10 What aspects of our modern world encourage and feed jealousy?

_____

_____

_____

11 How might jealousy and friendship with the world occur even in a church?

_____

_____

_____

12 What is involved in humbling yourself before God (4:7)?

_____

_____

_____

_____

13 Where have you sensed the devil's strongest attacks in your life recently? How can you resist him?

_____

_____

_____

14 Assuming that conflict is inevitable in this fallen world, what does it mean for believers to fight fairly?

_____

_____

_____

_____

15 How can you learn to fight fairly? How can you be less contentious?

_____

_____

_____

16 Think of all the people with whom you are at odds now. Can anything be done about these situations? List the relationships that you feel courageous enough to work on.

_____

_____

_____

_____

_____

17 Select one person from your list above. Keeping in mind the causes of disagreement mentioned by James, search your heart before God to see if one of them may be at the root of the problem. What could you do to begin to restore this relationship?

RESOLVE
to take action

_____

_____

_____

_____

_____

MORE
for studying
other themes
in this section

A What does James teach in this section that would help us have a more effective prayer life? What hinders our prayers (4:3)?

B Why does James call his audience "adulterers"? In what ways do believers today continue to be adulterous?

C How does humility square with celebrating what Christ has done for us (4:9-10)? What will happen if we do not humble ourselves?

D When is it permissible for Christians to judge one another (4:11-12)? What kind of judging is this passage talking about? When have you been guilty of judging?

LESSON 10
TALKING ABOUT TOMORROW
JAMES 4:13-17

REFLECT
on your life

1 Think back to grade school. What did you want to be when you grew up?

_____

_____

_____

2 What dreams do you have for the next five to ten years?

_____

_____

_____

READ
the passage

Read James 4:13-17 and the following notes:

❏ 4:13-16   ❏ 4:14   ❏ 4:17

3 What is the attitude behind the quote in 4:13? When have you recently heard someone talk like this?

_____

_____

_____

4 For what reason is a self-reliant approach to life foolish?

_____

_____

_____

5 The general statement about sins of omission in 4:17 is important on its own. How does it relate to planning for the future and boasting about tomorrow?

_____

_____

_____

_____

6 Why do Christians sometimes boast, brag, and make plans for their lives and work and yet give no thought to God?

REALIZE
the principle

_____

_____

_____

Many people say they believe in God but they are really practicing atheists. In the way they approach basic decisions and plan for the future, they live as if God didn't exist. They take no account of God's sustaining care or grace; they act as if they are self-sufficient and in control; and they take credit for all the good things they experience. Listening to them speak or watching them work, one would have no idea that God is a factor in their life. James, in his usual candid way, simply calls this attitude foolish, sinful, and evil. How much better to actively recognize God's right to order and direct our life as he pleases. If you have given your life to Christ, have you also given him your future?

7 Self-reliance and independence rightfully belong to God alone. Why do believers, and churches for that matter, so often want to take matters into their own hands?

_____

_____

_____

_____

8 Give some examples of planning or talking about the future in a way that leaves God out of the picture.

RESPOND
to the message

_____

_____

_____

_____

9 What are some past decisions in either your personal life or the life of your church where you now wonder whether God was left out of the picture?

_____

_____

_____

_____

_____

10 Some people forget about God when it comes to financial planning. When do you tend to leave God out of the picture?

_____

_____

_____

_____

11 We have all heard people boast about their future plans. When are you most tempted to boast? What might you be trying to gain through this?

_____

_____

_____

_____

_____

12 What causes you to set goals and plan for the future with little regard for God?

_____

_____

_____

_____

13 What personal warning signs indicate you are leaving God out of the picture? In what situations should you be alert to this?

_____

_____

_____

_____

14 How is it possible to plan and set specific goals for the future so that God is pleased and honored?

_____

_____

_____

_____

15 When do you next expect to be talking about your plans for the future (with spouse, friends, or co-workers)? How will you avoid boasting and leaving God out of the picture?

RESOLVE
to take action

_____

_____

_____

_____

_____

16 Determine how you can answer the question of what you are going to do next week or next year. Some people say, "God willing . . ." and others say, "If the Lord wills . . . ." What is a natural way for you to bring God into your plans?

_____

_____

_____

A How is Jesus' prayer in the garden of Gethsemane (Luke 22:42-44) a model for submissive, believing prayer about the future?

MORE
for studying
other themes
in this section

B When can praying "If it is your will" indicate an unbelieving or weak attitude? What is the relationship between boldness and submission in your prayers?

C James teaches the general principle that whoever knows what to do and doesn't do it sins. Sins of omission need to be forgiven as much as sins of commission. In what areas of your life are you failing to do what you should?

LESSON 11
WHAT POSSESSES YOU?
JAMES 5:1-6

REFLECT
on your life

1 List any millionaires you can name.

_____

_____

_____

_____

2 Describe a time when you desperately wanted something but getting it ultimately led to a major disappointment. Why didn't this live up to your expectations? What did you learn from this experience?

_____

_____

_____

_____

_____

READ
the passage

Read James 5:1-6 and the following notes:

❏ 5:1-6   ❏ 5:6

3 How does James describe the lifestyle of the rich?

_____

_____

_____

_____

4 What is the effect of their lifestyle on others?

_____

_____

_____

_____

5 What is the effect of their lifestyle on themselves?

_____

_____

_____

_____

6 Who are these rich people—are they non-Christians or sinful Christians in the church?

_____

_____

_____

_____

7 What influences can blind people to the ultimate worthlessness of material possessions?

_____

REALIZE
the principle

_____

_____

_____

Jesus spent a lot of time talking about money because there is a close connection between the heart and material possessions. In Matthew 16:26, Jesus asked what it would benefit a man if he gained the whole world but lost his soul. In this passage, James makes the same point using powerful and dramatic images. It is nothing less than folly to value and pursue things that don't satisfy and won't last beyond the grave. These rich people were compounding that error by exploiting and manipulating people in pursuit of wealth. When material possessions become most important, people become expendable. If you have been blessed with riches, guard your heart so they don't become your god. If you find yourself being caught up in the pursuit of material possessions, hear the words of warning and perspective offered by James. Finally, if you have suffered under the hand of rich oppressors (even other believers), know that God has heard your cry and will dispense judgment in his time.

8 It has been said that one of Satan's strategies is to change the price tags while no one is looking so that people value the wrong things. In light of this, what do people tend to pursue that has little eternal value?

_____

_____

_____

_____

9 List some well-known people who seemed to have it all but were, in fact, impoverished.

_____

_____

_____

_____

10 Why does James speak so strongly against self-indulgence? What kinds of self-indulgent activities are "in" now? Why is this inappropriate for believers?

_____

_____

_____

_____

11 God gives you money for your needs and pleasure, and for his glory. What does it mean to offer all your resources, time, and gifts to God with open hands?

_____

_____

_____

_____

12 Are you investing time and money in anything that is not really worth much from an eternal perspective? If so, what?

_____

_____

_____

_____

13 What would be worth pursuing that you aren't?

_____

_____

_____

_____

14 How can you invest yourself even more in what will matter forever?

_____

_____

_____

_____

15 Write down one way that you intend to change your lifestyle to reflect eternal and imperishable values. Consider sharing this with a close friend who will pray with you and encourage you to be a doer and not just a hearer.

RESOLVE
to take action

_____

_____

_____

_____

A When will the ungodly rich receive the promised misery that is coming? How does the threat of impending judgment affect their lifestyle?

MORE
for studying
other themes
in this section

B Why does James refer to God as "the LORD of Heaven's Armies" (5:4)? What does this name mean? How should referring to God by this name affect our attitudes and behavior?

C Compare the descriptions of the rich in this passage with the parable of the rich man and Lazarus in Luke 16:19-31. How is this an encouragement?

LESSON 12
THOSE WHO WAIT
JAMES 5:7-12

R
REFLECT
on your life

1 As a child, what did you find difficult to wait for?

_____

_____

_____

2 What is the most patient animal you can think of?

_____

3 Who is the most patient person you know?

_____

4 Which Bible character do you admire for his or her patience? Why?

_____

_____

_____

R
READ
the passage

Read James 5:7-12 and the following notes:

❒ 5:7, 8   ❒ 5:9

5 How does this section relate to 5:1-6?

_____

_____

_____

6 Most people would advise fighting against suffering or doing all you can to escape it. Why is it important to be patient in suffering?

_____

_____

7 Describe Job's experience of perseverance. How is his example an encouragement for us?

_____

_____

_____

8 Why does a God full of tenderness and mercy allow his people to experience suffering?

_____

_____

REALIZE
the principle

This passage continues some themes that James has already expressed in this letter: that Christians are to live in light of eternity, that God can be trusted to give good gifts to his children, and that problems are to bring us to God rather than turn us against fellow Christians. These truths have great value as we experience injustice and as we suffer in an evil world. Though the world might counsel self-defense, vengeance, and warfare, God counsels patience. The patience described here is rooted in an assurance of better things from God; it is confident that God is in control and is for us; it sees all the experience in this life in light of eternity. Whenever you feel discouraged, bitter, or ready to do battle, step back and offer it all to God. Ask him to help you persevere in your faith.

9 What is the role of faith in responding to suffering?

_____

_____

_____

10 What is the difference between patience and perseverance? Which is more difficult for you?

RESPOND
to the message

_____

_____

_____

11 In what ways do Christians still suffer for their faith?

_____

_____

_____

12 Why should the upcoming day of judgment be an incentive for patient living now?

_____

_____

_____

13 What is most difficult for you about being patient in suffering?

_____

_____

_____

_____

14 Think about a situation in which you have suffered. How could you have been more patient at that time?

_____

_____

_____

_____

_____

15 What will prevent patience from becoming laziness and inactivity? How is it possible to be patient and yet active?

_____

_____

_____

16 How might persevering in suffering bring blessing to you (5:11)?

_____

_____

_____

17 Select one aspect of your life in which you are experiencing suffering. How patient are you in this suffering? What would it mean to be even more patient?

RESOLVE
to take action

_____

_____

_____

_____

_____

A Which prophets were good examples of patience? What was their secret?

MORE
for studying
other themes
in this section

B When is it difficult for a farmer to be patient? What happens to impatient farmers?

C What influence should the Lord's imminent return have on how we live (5:8)?

D Why was James concerned about oath taking (5:12)? Why is it so difficult to believe another's simple yes or no? Why is this important for believers?

LESSON 13
REAL POWER
JAMES 5:13-20

REFLECT
on your life

1 Describe a time when God clearly answered your prayers.

_____

_____

_____

_____

2 What is your most memorable experience in prayer with others?

_____

_____

_____

_____

_____

READ
the passage

Read James 5:13-20 and the following notes:

❏ 5:14, 15   ❏ 5:15   ❏ 5:16   ❏ 5:16-18   ❏ 5:19, 20

3 What can be accomplished through prayer?

_____

_____

_____

_____

4 What are the elements of powerful and effective prayer?

_____

_____

_____

_____

5 Why does James point to Elijah as an example of prayer (5:17-18)?

_____

_____

_____

_____

6 How does the attitude of confidence and certainty regarding prayer in these verses relate to James 4:15?

_____

_____

_____

_____

7 Why do so many believers consider prayer as a last resort?

_____

_____

_____

_____

REALIZE
the principle

James describes believing prayer as a dynamic and powerful activity of the Christian life. It is an instrument of healing and forgiveness, and a mighty weapon for spiritual warfare. However, for some Christians, prayer is little more than a comfortable ritual that has few demands and offers even fewer rewards. People with this perspective need to read James with fresh eyes and an open heart. Other people mistakenly view prayer as a way to obligate God to give them whatever they claim in faith, as if God were a heavenly vending machine! They need to remember that though God is pleased to use our prayers to accomplish his purposes, and though he delights in responding in love to our requests, he is never bound by our prayers. As you come to the Father in faith, praying in accordance with his will, prayer will be the single most effective ministry you can have. Never apologize to someone for "just" being able to pray. When you pray, you give the best you have to give.

8 What could be some of God's reasons for not answering prayers in our way or in our time?

_____

_____

_____

9 Does God always grant the requests of spiritual people? What people do you know who seem unusually effective in prayer?

_____

_____

_____

10 How would you characterize the prayer life of your church?

_____

_____

_____

11 Do you prefer to pray with others or by yourself? What would happen if one of these is consistently neglected in the life of a believer?

_____

_____

_____

12 How satisfied are you with your prayer life?

_____

_____

_____

13 What would motivate you to pray more frequently and with more earnestness?

_____

_____

_____

14 Talk with some members of your church about ways to increase your church's use of prayer in building God's kingdom. How could a church help its members pray more effectively? Make a covenant together to practice one specific idea.

RESOLVE
to take action

_____

_____

_____

_____

_____

A What is the use and value of oil in praying for the sick (5:14)? What does this mean for us?

MORE
for studying
other themes
in this section

B If Jesus is our only mediator and forgives our sins, why does James tell us to confess our sins to each other?

C How do we know when someone has wandered from the truth (5:19)? What should we do if that person does not want to have anything to do with us?

D For what situations would you recommend that someone read the book of James? How would you sum up the main benefits for believers from studying this book?

Take Your Bible Study to the Next Level

The **Life Application Study Bible** helps you apply truths in God's Word to everyday life. It's packed with nearly 10,000 notes and features that make it today's #1–selling study Bible.

Life Application Notes: Thousands of Life Application notes help explain God's Word and challenge you to apply the truth of Scripture to your life.

Personality Profiles: You can benefit from the life experiences of over a hundred Bible figures.

Book Introductions: These provide vital statistics, an overview, and a timeline to help you quickly understand the message of each book.

Maps: Over 200 maps next to the Bible text highlight important Bible places and events.

Christian Worker's Resource: Enhance your ministry effectiveness with this practical supplement.

Charts: Over 260 charts help explain difficult concepts and relationships.

Harmony of the Gospels: Using a unique numbering system, the events from all four Gospels are harmonized into one chronological account.

Daily Reading Plan: This reading plan is your guide to reading through the entire Bible in one unforgettable year.

Topical Index: A master index provides instant access to Bible passages and features that address the topics on your mind.

Dictionary/Concordance: With entries for many of the important words in the Bible, this is an excellent starting place for studying the Bible text.

Available in the New Living Translation, New International Version, King James Version, and New King James Version. Take an interactive tour of the *Life Application Study Bible* at
www.NewLivingTranslation.com/LASB

CP0271